USBORNE
DICTIONARY
of HORSES
& PONIES

Struan Reid
Consultant: Karen Bush

Designed by Linda Penny and Lindy Dark
Illustrated by Aziz Khan

Managing editor: Jane Chisholm

Managing designer: Stephen Wright

Contents

Introduction

This book is a comprehensive guide to all aspects of horses and ponies, and the words and phrases used to describe them. It begins with an account of their evolution and ancestry, and a history of their domestication. It looks at their instincts and anatomy, teeth, "points", conformation, and colors. The main breeds of ponies and horses are listed and described.

You can find out about saddles and fittings, horse care and styles of riding, training and bad behavior, as well as activities such as show jumping and racing. You can also learn about some of the famous horses in history, religion and in literature.

Here are just some of the things you can find out about in this dictionary.

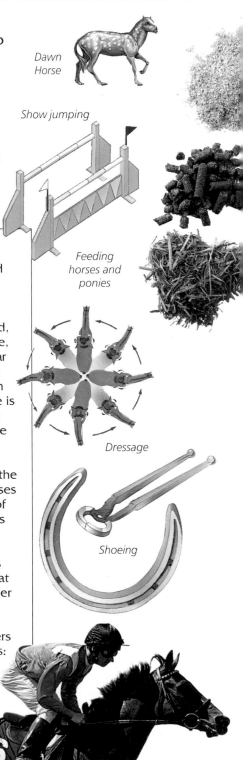

Dawn Horse

Show jumping

Feeding horses and ponies

Dressage

Shoeing

Racing

Barns and stalls

Bridles and bits

Skeleton

Using this book

This reference book is arranged thematically under specific subject headings.

Wherever a word, phrase or topic is introduced or explained, the word is printed in bold type, like this: **foal**. Where an unfamiliar word is explained in more detail on another page, it is printed in italic type, like this: *foal**. There is a footnote at the bottom of the page showing where to find the full explanation.

Toward the end of the book you can find a list of some of the important events held for horses and ponies in different parts of the world, and useful addresses that can be contacted for more information.

A section on extra horse terms contains definitions of words that have not been explained earlier in the book, as well as other useful words.

In the index, the page numbers which are in bold type, like this: **15**, show where the main explanation for the entry can be found in the book.

The evolution of the horse

The horse belongs to a species of animal called **Equus caballus** whose history goes back a million years. Other members of the family include asses, zebras and onagers. But in order to look at the horse's earliest ancestors, we have to go back even further - about 60 million years.

Ass

Onager

Zebra

The dawn horse

The modern horse is descended from **Eohippus**, known as the "dawn horse", which first appeared about 60 million years ago. It was about the size of a fox and didn't look like a modern horse at all. When fossils of it were first discovered, it was named **Hyracotherium**, or the "hyrax beast".

• The dawn horse had four toes on each of its front feet and three on its back feet, like the tapir of today.
• Remains of its teeth indicate that it chewed leaves rather than grass.

Later stages

The dawn horse developed into two types, known as **Mesohippus** and **Miohippus**. Both these animals had three toes on all four feet, and they were slightly larger than the dawn horse. They also had more efficient teeth, so that they could eat more food.

• A later stage was **Merychippus**. This developed into six separate lines, of which **Pliohippus** is the most important. It was from this animal that *Equus caballus* itself evolved, about 1 million years ago.
• As the horse family developed, other minor changes in the size of its body and the structure of its legs enabled it to run faster. There were also changes in the size and number of teeth which eventually enabled it to graze grass.

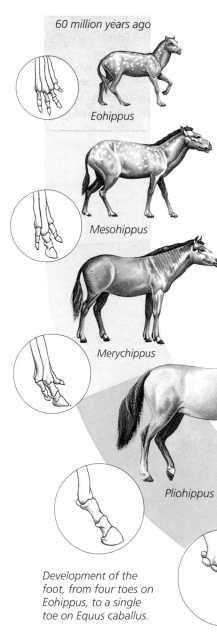

60 million years ago

Eohippus

Mesohippus

Merychippus

Pliohippus

Development of the foot, from four toes on Eohippus, to a single toe on Equus caballus.

Equus caballus

1 million years ago

For a link to a website where you can visit a virtual horse museum where you can find out how horses evolved, go to **www.usborne-quicklinks.com**

Migration and disappearance

A number of fossil skeletons of the earliest stages in the development of *Equus caballus* have been found in North America. They show that the horse first appeared and developed there.

• These early horses crossed over land bridges to Asia and then on to Africa and Europe.

• Then, for some unknown reason, a few thousand years ago, the horse died out in America. It was not seen there again until it was reintroduced by European settlers in the 16th century.

Fossil of an early horse

Przewalski's horse *Tarpan*

Two direct ancestors

Two forms of *Equus caballus* survived the Ice Age **Przewalski's horse**, which still exists, and the **Tarpan**, which was hunted to extinction by the end of the 19th century. These two are believed to be the ancestors of the *Arab** and other Oriental breeds of horse.

• The Tarpan was the type of horse used by early chariot-driving people of the eastern Mediterranean. It has now been "reconstructed" by selective breeding in Poland.

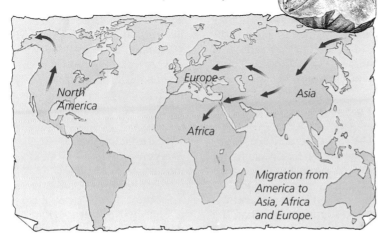

North America

Europe

Asia

Africa

Migration from America to Asia, Africa and Europe.

Landscape and climate

Landscape and climate have played an important part in the development of the horse since the last Ice Age over 10,000 years ago. Different conditions have produced the many different types of horses that can be found throughout the world today.

• Generally, **hot climates** turned out tall, elegant horses.

• **Cold** and **mountainous regions** produced small, compact horses, today known as *ponies**.

• **Dry areas** with little grazing produced light, agile animals.

• **Wetter areas** with lush grazing encouraged large, *heavy horses** to develop.

Warm bloods and cold bloods

Some people believe that *light horses** descend from Przewalski's horse and the Tarpan. They are known as **"warm-blooded"**.

Steppe horse (warm-blooded)

• Heavy horses, called **"cold-blooded"**, descend from the **Forest horse**.

Forest horse

• Many modern breeds are a mixture of both warm- and cold-blooded breeds.

*Arab, 28; Heavy horses, 32; Light horse, 120; Pony, 14

The domestication of the horse

For a long time, horses were too fast and quick-witted for people to catch them. They were first hunted and caught for food about 20-30,000 years ago, when people began to learn about their seasonal migrations.

From hunted to helper

At first horses were hunted and caught for food. Later they were tamed, so that people could ride and breed them. The first people to do this were nomadic horsemen from Central Asia, some time before 2500BC. The first tame horses were small, and were herded like cattle and kept for their milk, meat and skins. Later, they were also trained and used for transporting people, for pulling heavy loads, and for farming.

Cave painting of a wild horse, about 12000BC

New equipment

Ancient cave painting of a horse in harness

The more people used horses, the more control they needed over them.
• Early riders would probably have used *bridles** of some kind, but no equipment used on these early domesticated horses has survived.

• The earliest known *nosebands** and *bits** come from **Gaza** in Palestine and date from the 14th century BC. One example is a bronze bit with a plain bar mouthpiece and wheel-shaped cheekpieces with spikes on their inner surfaces.
• The most elaborate ancient bits date from the 10th-7th centuries BC, and come from **Luristan** in western Iran. They have straight mouthpieces and ends cast in shapes such as horses, gods and monsters.

Some of the earliest surviving bits used on horses

• *Saddles** were probably first used by the **Sarmatians** of Central Asia, in the 3rd century BC.

Felt picture of horseman in early saddle

Their saddles were built high at the front and back, to hold the horseman and provide a base against which he could brace his back.

With the use of horses and saddles, the cavalry became the most important part of an army.

For a link to a website where you can explore an interactive reconstruction of an Iron Age chariot found in a grave, go to **www.usborne-quicklinks.com**

Hittite charioteers. One drove, while the other fought.

The warhorse

By the end of the Bronze Age, about 3,000 years ago, horses had become very important in **warfare**.

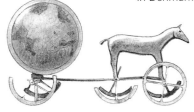

Bronze model known as the Solar Wagon, from Trundholm in Denmark

• The introduction of warhorses pulling **chariots** changed the art of warfare and the balance of power in the ancient world. For many centuries horse-drawn chariots were the most effective weapons on the battlefield.

• The master charioteers of the ancient world were the **Hittites** of eastern Turkey. From 1450BC, they carved out a huge empire from the Mediterranean to the Persian Gulf. Their success was largely due to their use of horses and the skill of their charioteers.

A change of weapons

Gradually the use of horses and chariots in battle declined. This was because missile weapons such as **bows** and **arrows** were being used more and more. This made the charioteers far more vulnerable to attacks from foot soldiers. So the nature of warfare changed once more.

Cavalry

In order to cope with these new weapons, a more flexible fighting force was needed. Horses began to be used as chargers, ridden by armored soldiers. This became known as **cavalry**.

Chinese soldier with bow and arrows

Horses were bred in increasing numbers to cope with this new role.

• The **Assyrians** (from Iraq) were probably the first people to use cavalry in warfare, from about 720 BC. Their horsemen acted either as archers or spearmen. They rode without saddles, sitting in the center of the horse's back, with their knees up. The Assyrians conquered a huge empire with an army of 60,000 soldiers, 2,000 of which were cavalry.

Carving of an Assyrian horseman in a royal hunt, dating to the 17th century BC

Chinese stone carving of a horse with stirrups

• *Stirrups** were first used by the **Huns** of Mongolia in the 4th century AD.

Stirrups supported the rider's feet and enabled him to charge down on his enemy with more force.

Stirrups also gave the rider more control over his horse. This enabled people to travel greater distances than before and more horses began to be used.

Stirrups were not commonly used in Europe until the 9th century.

Bits, 40; Bridles, 38; Nosebands, 39; Saddles, 34; Stirrups, 37

Horses' minds

A horse's mentality is based on instincts which have developed over thousands of years, as a means of survival among dangers in the wild. Horses also have very sharp senses and an elaborate system of communication with other horses.

The herd instinct

A horse's survival in the wild depended on being part of a herd. Horses have a very strong **herd instinct**. This is the inborn tendency to associate with others.

A small herd of horses

Even with domesticated horses, the herd instinct is the strongest of all their characteristics and it still plays an important part. Horses need the company of others, and often feel vulnerable on their own.

A horse that is usually calm with other horses can become difficult when on his own. Another animal, such as a donkey, can help.

Using the herd instinct

People can make use of a horse's herd instinct. For example, if a horse is nervous of something, a more experienced horse can be used to give him a lead and make him confident.

Leadership

Wild horses have a **leader**. Domesticated horses usually have a "pecking order". Some personalities are more dominant, while others are more submissive.

Senses

Horses have very acute senses. This affects their personalities, and how they react to their surroundings.

Touch

Parts of a horse's body are very sensitive to **touch**. He

will become more confident with a strange object by touching it with his muzzle.

Taste

Taste is allied to the sense of smell. Horses have sensitive palates and they quickly reject food they do not like.

Sight

Horses' eyes are placed on either side of the head. This gives a very wide **field of vision**, much wider at the sides than that of people. When the horse raises his head, it is also possible for him to see nearly all the way behind as well.

View with both eyes

Vision of left eye

Vision of right eye

Blind

A horse is able to see all but a small area directly behind him.

Smell

A horse's sense of smell is very sharp.

Their sense of **smell** helps horses to detect predators and find and select suitable food. Strange and unusual smells or unpleasant ones may make them nervous.

Hearing

Horses' **hearing** is very sharp. Their ears are placed on top of their heads and are very mobile. A horse can move them around and direct them toward sounds. Their shape helps to collect the sounds.

For a link to a website where you can learn a lot more about your pony, including how it communicates, go to **www.usborne-quicklinks.com**

Communication

Horses communicate with each other with calls, but also by the position and movement of their bodies. This is called **body language**. They have developed an elaborate system of signs, and they watch each other carefully for these signals.

Calls

The **neigh** is a contact and recognition call. There are many differences between horses' neighs. They can recognize members of their group by their neighs. A **whinny** is a gentle neigh.

Tails and ears

Tail and ear movements are clear means of signaling.
• The **higher the tail**, the more aroused the horse.
• A **lashing tail** shows annoyance and irritation.
• **Ears that droop** show a lack of attention, while **ears forward** indicate attention.
• **Ears laid flat** back is a sign of anger, pain or fear.

Mouths

Mouth movements are a way of communicating among horses.
• **Lips drawn back** to show teeth and gums indicate submission.

• A **tight mouth** can indicate tension (fear or anger). Usually the more relaxed a horse or pony is, the more relaxed his mouth will be.

Noses

Noses are often used to communicate.
• **Flared nostrils** indicate arousal, as in fear or surprise.
• **Nose wrinkling** shows annoyance or disgust.

Head movements

• The **head thrust**, in which the nose is jerked sharply forward and upward, is the most common threatening sign between horses.
• A slower, gentler **nudge** is a friendly movement.
• **Head shakes** up and down can indicate annoyance or frustration.
• The **nose shake** is often done by stallions *displaying**.
• The **jerk-back** is an abrupt upward and inward movement. This indicates fear or dislike.

Neck movements

• The **neck swing** moves the horse's head away from a threat of danger.
• **Head snaking** is a sign of aggression and dominance. The horse stretches his head out low and moves it from side to side.

Body movements

• The **body check**, when a horse swings in front of another, is a warning.
• A **shoulder barge** is full contact and a warning.
• **Rump presentation** is a mild threat to kick.

Legs

• The **hindleg lift** is a strong threat to kick.
• The **foreleg strike** is a warning to keep away.
• **Pawing** is used to investigate things and is also a sign of frustration.

Attack and defense

• An **aggressive** move is made head-on.

• A **defensive** move is made rear-on.

*Display, 119

9

Points of the horse

Horses' bodies are designed for strength and speed, but some are stronger or faster than others. The different parts of a horse's body are known as the **points**, and many have special names. This makes it easy to refer to particular areas without confusion.

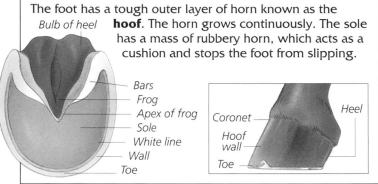

Points of the foot

The foot has a tough outer layer of horn known as the **hoof**. The horn grows continuously. The sole has a mass of rubbery horn, which acts as a cushion and stops the foot from slipping.

Bulb of heel
Bars
Frog
Apex of frog
Sole
White line
Wall
Toe

Coronet
Heel
Hoof wall
Toe

Points of the horse

Although there are many different breeds of horses and ponies, they all belong to the same species - *Equus caballus** - and share the same points of the body.

Mane Crest Neck Poll Forelock
Ears
Shoulder
Quarters Point
Croup of hip Loins Back Withers
Dock Hip
joint
Point of
buttock
Eye
Thigh
Throat
Cheek
Windpipe
Chin groove
Point of
shoulder Muzzle
Chest Nostril
Sheath Elbow
Flank
Stifle Belly
Point of hock Chestnut Forearm
Hock
Tail Knee
Shannon Fetlock joints
Cannon bone
Fetlock
Ergot Pastern Pastern
Hoof Coronet

*Equus caballus, 4

For a link to a website where you can play a fun online game to test yourself on the different parts of a horse's body, go to **www.usborne-quicklinks.com**

The horse's muscles

The **muscles** on the body of a horse or pony provide the power to drive the animal forward, so they need to be large and strong. They are made up of thousands of fibers which expand and bend to give movement. Each muscle is attached to the part of the body it is responsible for moving. Most muscles work in groups or pairs.

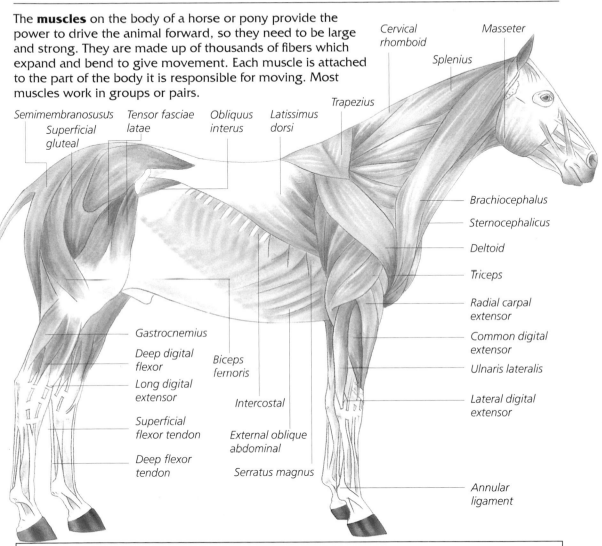

Cervical rhomboid

Masseter

Splenius

Trapezius

Semimembranosusus

Superficial gluteal

Tensor fasciae latae

Obliquus interus

Latissimus dorsi

Brachiocephalus

Sternocephalicus

Deltoid

Triceps

Radial carpal extensor

Gastrocnemius

Common digital extensor

Deep digital flexor

Biceps femoris

Ulnaris lateralis

Long digital extensor

Intercostal

Lateral digital extensor

Superficial flexor tendon

External oblique abdominal

Deep flexor tendon

Serratus magnus

Annular ligament

Leg muscles and tendons

Muscles are attached to bones by strong cords called **tendons**. The flexor muscles and tendons bend the legs, while the extensors project them forward. There are no muscles below the knees and hocks, so long tendons connect the muscles to the lower legs and the feet.

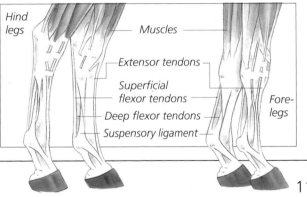

Hind legs

Muscles

Extensor tendons

Superficial flexor tendons

Deep flexor tendons

Suspensory ligament

Fore-legs

11

The horse's skeleton

The horse's **skeleton** is the main framework of its body. It supports the body and protects the most delicate organs inside: the skull shields the brain, while the ribs guard the heart, lungs and organs. The bones are connected by movable joints and worked by muscles. Fossils show how the horse's skeleton has adapted over 60 million years, from the earliest *Eohippus** (dawn horse), to the modern horse *Equus caballus**.

The bones of the skeleton

There are two main parts to a horse's skeleton. The **axial skeleton** protects the horse's vital parts and consists of the skull, the ribcage and the backbone. The **appendicular skeleton** supports the body and consists of the shoulders and forelegs, pelvis and hind legs.

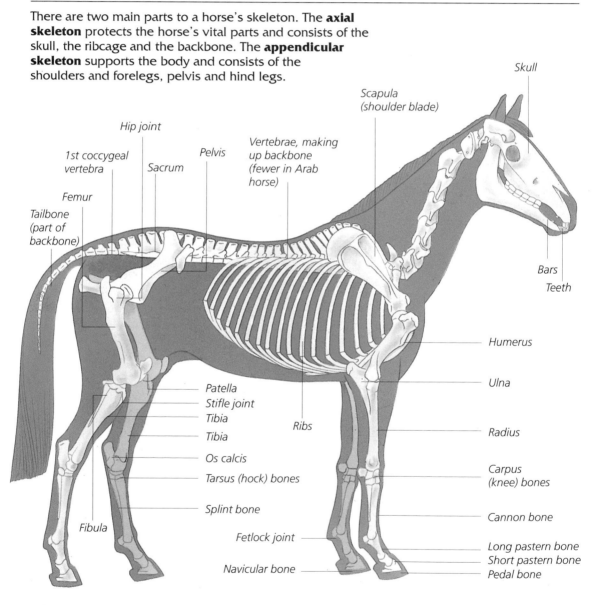

Skull

Scapula (shoulder blade)

Hip joint

1st coccygeal vertebra

Pelvis

Vertebrae, making up backbone (fewer in Arab horse)

Sacrum

Femur

Tailbone (part of backbone)

Bars

Teeth

Humerus

Ulna

Patella
Stifle joint
Tibia

Ribs

Tibia

Radius

Os calcis

Tarsus (hock) bones

Carpus (knee) bones

Splint bone

Cannon bone

Fibula

Fetlock joint

Long pastern bone
Short pastern bone
Pedal bone

Navicular bone

*Eohippus, 4; Equus caballus, 4

Axial skeleton

The skull protects the brain. The backbone carries and protects the spinal cord. The ribcage protects the heart, lungs and other important internal organs.

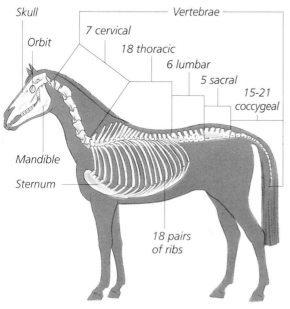

Skull

Orbit

7 cervical

Vertebrae

18 thoracic

6 lumbar

5 sacral

15-21 coccygeal

Mandible

Sternum

18 pairs of ribs

Appendicular skeleton

This part of the horse's skeleton supports the rest of its body. The shoulders, pelvis, fore and hind legs are connected to the axial skeleton through a network of muscles and ligaments.

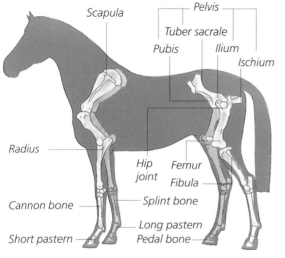

Scapula

Pelvis

Tuber sacrale

Pubis

Ilium

Ischium

Radius

Hip joint

Femur

Fibula

Cannon bone

Splint bone

Long pastern

Short pastern

Pedal bone

Human skeleton

The human skeleton has a number of features in common with that of the horse. But humans and horses have evolved to meet different survival needs - the horse to run fast on four legs, the human to stand upright on two legs.

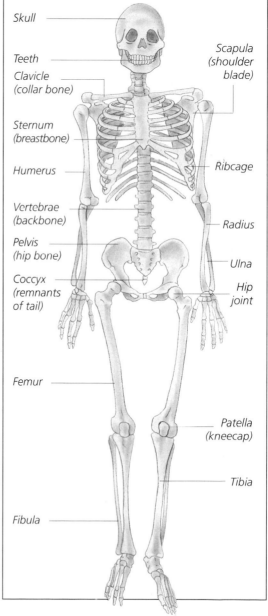

Skull

Teeth

Clavicle (collar bone)

Sternum (breastbone)

Humerus

Vertebrae (backbone)

Pelvis (hip bone)

Coccyx (remnants of tail)

Femur

Fibula

Scapula (shoulder blade)

Ribcage

Radius

Ulna

Hip joint

Patella (kneecap)

Tibia

Describing a horse

There are a number of vital statistics which give the basic information about the height, age and sex of a horse or pony. When buying a horse or pony, there are a number of points to consider before the final choice is made. First of all, the buyer will have to decide not only that the animal looks right, but also that his character is suitable.

Measurement

The height of a horse is usually given in **hands**. A hand is measured from the ground up to the highest point of the horse's *withers**.

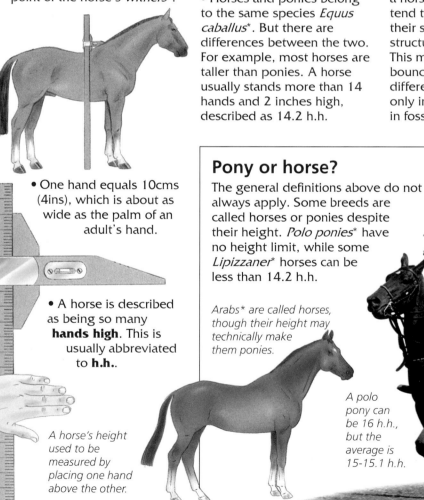

• One hand equals 10cms (4ins), which is about as wide as the palm of an adult's hand.

• A horse is described as being so many **hands high**. This is usually abbreviated to **h.h.**.

A horse's height used to be measured by placing one hand above the other.

What is a horse?

The word "horse" can be used as a general term to describe either a horse or pony, male or female.
• Horses and ponies belong to the same species *Equus caballus**. But there are differences between the two. For example, most horses are taller than ponies. A horse usually stands more than 14 hands and 2 inches high, described as 14.2 h.h.

What is a pony?

The proper definition of a **pony** is a male or female horse which stands 14.2 h.h. or less. Although they are smaller than horses, most ponies are stronger for their size than horses.

But ponies are probably not simply small horses. There are a number of different points of *conformation**, as well as differences in size, that distinguish a pony from a horse. For example, ponies tend to be more upright in their shoulders and in the structure of their lower legs. This makes them more bouncy to ride. These differences can be seen, not only in horses today, but also in fossil remains.

Pony or horse?

The general definitions above do not always apply. Some breeds are called horses or ponies despite their height. *Polo ponies** have no height limit, while some *Lipizzaner** horses can be less than 14.2 h.h.

Arabs* are called horses, though their height may technically make them ponies.

A polo pony can be 16 h.h., but the average is 15-15.1 h.h.

---

*Arab, 28; Equus caballus, 4; Conformation, 16; Lipizzaner, 31; Polo, 87; Withers, 10

For a link to a website where you can study an
online glossary of horse terms, go to
www.usborne-quicklinks.com

Age

• A **foal** is a young horse or pony up to the age of 1 year. It is described as either a **colt foal** (male) or a **filly foal** (female).

• A **filly** is a female horse or pony more than 1 year but less than 4 years old.

• A **colt** is a male horse which is over 1 year but less than 4 years old.

Foal

• A **yearling** is a horse aged between 1 and 2 years old. Depending on its sex, it is described as either a **yearling colt** or a **yearling filly**.

• As the name suggests, a **two-year-old** is a **two-year-old colt** or **filly**.

Yearling

Two-year-old

Sex

• A **mare** is a female horse which is four years old or more.

• A **gelding** is a male horse which has been **gelded**, or castrated. This means it has had its reproductive organs removed so that it cannot reproduce. Horses may be gelded from the age of six months onward.

• A **stallion** is an ungelded male horse aged 4 years or over, used for **stud** (breeding) purposes.

Which should you choose?

• Most male horses which are not going to be used for breeding purposes are gelded. This makes them easier to keep and to handle. Stallions are not suitable for novice, or inexperienced, owners and riders.

• Mares can sometimes require more tactful and patient riding and handling than geldings, especially when they are "in season" during the breeding season (spring to summer). At this time they become more sensitive and are easily upset.

• Geldings are generally more tolerant and easy-going than other horses.

• Although some people have preferences as to the sex of their horse, it is more important that each animal should be judged on its individual merits and its suitability for the buyer.

It is important to choose the horse or pony that suits you best.

15

Conformation

Conformation is the term used to describe the physical characteristics of a horse or pony. The ideal conformation varies according to the breed of pony or horse. But there are many points of conformation common to all breeds.

Good conformation

The better the conformation, the more likely the horse or pony is to stay healthy. Good conformation will make him easier to train and able to work more efficiently. No horse or pony has perfect conformation, and you can disregard minor faults as long as they do not affect the animal's performance or health.

Head

A horse's **head** should be in proportion to his size. It should not be too long or heavy, as this affects his movement.

Poll

Eyes are large and well-spaced.

Good width between jaw bones.

• The angle at which the head joins the neck is important. If it is too sharp it can squeeze the *larynx** and affect breathing. But if the angle is too wide, the horse will find it difficult to flex, or bend, at the poll.
• Large, wide **nostrils** are important as they allow a good intake of air.

• A *convex** or **Roman nose** is sometimes found in horses who have *heavy horse** blood.

• A *concave** profile or **dish face** indicates *Arab** blood.

Ears

Ears should be neat and perky, alert and usually held forward (or "pricked").
• Slightly curly ears are often seen on Arabs. Some riders believe they show lots of character and are attractive.

Eyes

Eyes should be large and clear, giving a direct, kind look and calm expression. Should be set wide apart for a wide range of vision, with a broad forehead.

Neck

The **neck** should be in proportion to the rest of the body, with a convex curve from poll to withers.

Chest

The **chest** should be wide enough to give plenty of room for the heart and lungs.

Forelegs

Viewed from the front, a line through the **forelegs** should go straight down from the point of shoulder, through the knee and cannon bone, to foot.
• The **elbows** should be held away from the body, so that they allow free movement.
• The **forearm** should be long and well-muscled.
• The **knees** should be large as the broad surfaces will absorb shock better.
• *Cannon bones** should have a good circumference and plenty of bone. They should be short and strong.

All legs

• The *fetlocks** should look flat, rather than rounded.
• **Pasterns** should have the same slope as the hoof: 45° in the front feet, and about 50° to 55° in the back feet. Pasterns which are upright are not as good at absorbing shock. This will lead to jarring, or concussion, of the legs, especially at the joints.

Pastern

On the front feet, the pasterns should slope at an angle of 45°.

45°

For a link to a website where you can read detailed information about the conformation of the American Saddlebred horse and see pictures as well, go to **www.usborne-quicklinks.com**

Feet

Feet should be neat and round and point straight forward. If they point outward or inward, they can cause uneven wear on the *shoes** and stress to the joints.

- Each pair should slope at the same angle and be the same size. Heels should be wide, *frogs** large to absorb concussion, and the soles should be slightly concave.

Good movement

From front and back, when walking and trotting, the horse should move straight and relaxed, with the hind feet directly following in the path of the forefeet. There should be no risk of the horse hitting his own legs through bad movement.

From the side, the horse should walk in an easy and comfortable style; the hind feet should **overtrack**, or overstep, the imprint of the forefeet.

Shoulders

Shoulders should be broad and slope well back from the point of the shoulder up to the withers. This makes the stride long and comfortable.

The slope of the shoulder should be roughly the same as the angle of the pastern.

Withers

45°

Withers

The **withers** should be well-defined and of a reasonable height. If they are too high or too low, they can cause the saddle to slip under the rider, or to rub the horse's skin.

The ribs should curve away from the backbone, to give plenty of room for the lungs to expand and for the digestive system.

45°

Back

Both the **back** and **loins** should be short and strong. This produces the strong muscles needed for jumping and galloping.

Girth

Girth (width around belly) should be in proportion. The body should be deepest just behind the elbows.

Hindquarters

Hindquarters should be strong and muscular to produce the power to move the horse. They should be rounded, but not slope too sharply to the tail.

- From behind, the muscles should curve out on either side, and turn in under the tail.

Hind legs

The **hind legs** should be powerful, as they move the horse forward. The point of hock should be directly below the point of buttock.

Hocks

The *hocks** are the hardest-worked of all the joints in the horse's body. From front to back, they should be large and wide to make the horse more flexible and balanced.

*Frog, 10; Hocks, 10; Shoes, 56   17

Conformation

Faults in conformation

Poor conformation will make a horse work less efficiently than one that is well-built, and it will also be harder for him to stay fit and healthy. Horses and ponies stand on their legs for much of their lives. They often rest standing up. So poor conformation will affect them when they are resting as well as working.

Small eyes

Small eyes lying close together can show a difficult

character. A **narrow forehead** also means there is less space for the nasal air passages.

Ears

Ears should also be looked at. **Long ears** are said to indicate speed, but ears permanently **laid flat** can indicate a bad temper.

Parrot mouth

A **parrot mouth** is an upper jaw in which the front teeth overhang the lower ones. Also known as **overshot**. In a bad case, it can prevent a horse from eating properly, which can lead to illness.

Ewe neck

A **ewe neck** has a weak crest (top) of the neck with strong muscles below. Horses with this fault often **poke their noses**, or **star gaze**, making it difficult for the riders to control them.

Bull neck

A **bull neck** is short and thick. It reduces flexibility at the *poll**.

Flat withers

Flat withers cause the saddle to slip and slide forward. This fault is often seen in ponies.

Upright shoulder

An **upright shoulder** gives good power for pulling. But it produces a short stride and jarring movement, giving an uncomfortable ride and damaging limbs and feet.

Goose rump

With a **goose rump**, the hindquarters slope sharply down from the highest point to the dock. But a horse with this may be a good jumper - it is sometimes known as **jumper's bump**.

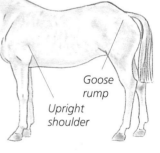

Goose rump

Upright shoulder

Short back

A **short back** may be strong, but a very short back can be difficult to fit a saddle to.

Long back

A **long back** is often narrow and weak, and it may be more prone to injury.

Roach back

A **roach back** curves upward. It may be badly formed or caused by injury.

Sway back

A **sway back** dips behind the withers. It shows old age or damaged vertebrae and is weak.

Overwide chest

A chest that is too wide is often described as **bosomy**. This makes a horse roll from side to side when going fast, giving a poor ride. Some broad-chested horses also have their forelegs set too far in underneath them, so that their balance is affected.

Tails

A **tail carried to one side** or **held low down** can indicate a back injury. A **swishing tail** can show a nervous temperament.

Poor movement

- If a horse's legs are thrown outward in a circular movement as he walks, this is known as **paddling**. Young horses that are weak or unsteady may paddle slightly. The condition may improve as the horse's muscles develop with work and age. Good *shoeing** can sometimes correct the problem.

- Another faulty movement is **winding**. The horse swings his feet inward, so that his steps are almost on a single line. A young horse can usually grow out of this as the muscles strengthen. It can be eased by good shoeing.

Back at the knee

If from the side a horse's forelegs look concave, it has a condition called "**back at the knee**", or sometimes "**calf knees**". This adds extra strain to the knees and the lower part of the legs.

Over at the knee

"**Over at the knee**", or "**standing over**", is the opposite to "back at the knee". In small degrees, this fault puts only a little strain on the tendons. But in bad cases, it can cause the horse to stumble. In an older horse the problem may be caused by too much wear and tear on the legs.

Sickle hocks

Sickle or **bent hocks** lead to a lack of power in the hind limbs. Hock joints and ligaments can be easily strained.

Cow hocks

With **cow hocks**, the toes are turned out and the hocks are turned in. This makes the legs move outward, instead of forward and in a straight line.

Upright pasterns

Upright pasterns are poor shock absorbers. They will give the rider an uncomfortable ride.

Long pasterns

Long pasterns cause strain on the tendons and ligaments of legs.

Pigeon toes

Pigeon toes occur when the front feet turn inward. Can lead to winding and strain. Hereditary or they can be caused by bad shoeing.

Boxy feet

Small, upright donkey-like feet, known as **boxy feet**, are poor at absorbing shock. This can lead to foot problems.

Flat feet

Large, open **flat feet** often have heels that are too low.

They can bruise easily. Horses with this type of feet can have problems walking on rough surfaces.

*Shoeing, 56

Teeth and aging

Horses, like people, have two sets of teeth: **temporary teeth**, also known as **milk teeth**, and **permanent teeth**. The milk teeth are smaller, smoother and whiter than the permanent adult teeth that replace them. The adult teeth are strong, large and yellowish in color. By the time a horse is six years old, he will have a full set of permanent teeth.

Arrangement of the horse's teeth

The horse has six front teeth in the upper jaw, and six in the lower jaw. These are called **incisors** (biting teeth). The pair in the middle are called **centrals**. The next pair on either side are the **laterals**, and the outer teeth are called **corners**. Behind the incisors lie the powerful **molars** (cheek teeth), which are used to grind up food. An adult horse has 24 permanent molars, while an immature horse has only 12 temporary molars.

Molars
Wolf teeth
Tushes
Incisors

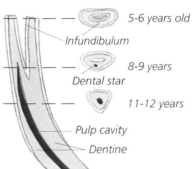

A horse's lower jaw. The front teeth (incisors) bite off grass, while the back teeth (molars) chew it.

Molars   Tushes
Corners
Laterals
Centrals

Tooth tables

As a horse grows older, the **tables** (biting surfaces) of the incisors are worn away. This reveals different parts of their inside structure. Incisor tables can give an idea of a horse's age (see opposite page).

5-6 years old
Infundibulum
8-9 years
Dental star
11-12 years
Pulp cavity
Dentine

Longitudinal section of incisor tooth

Growth and wear

When the permanent teeth are fully grown, a horse is said to have a **full mouth**. The age of a horse can be determined from his teeth while they are growing. But from the age of eight, when the permanent teeth are fully grown, assessing age from teeth becomes more difficult.

At birth, or within 2 weeks: The foal has two central incisors in each jaw. The laterals appear at 4-6 weeks, and the corners appear at 6-9 months old.

One year: Full set of incisor milk teeth, six in each jaw.

Two years: Six incisors in each jaw, and they are now all "in wear".

Two and a half years: The central incisors (two in each jaw) fall out, and permanent incisors appear.

Three years: Central incisors now fully grown and in wear.

Three and a half years: Milk laterals in each jaw replaced by permanent laterals.

For a link to a website where you can find out more about horses' teeth, go to **www.usborne-quicklinks.com**

Four years: Lateral incisors now fully grown and in wear.

Four and a half years: Milk corners in each jaw replaced by permanent corners.

Four-five years: In male horses (and sometimes in females too) small pointed teeth called **tushes** appear behind the corners in the lower jaw.

Five years: Corner incisors now fully grown and in wear.

Six years: Horse now has a full mouth of permanent teeth, which are said to be "in use".

Seven years: A hook appears on the corner teeth of the upper jaw. (A similar hook may show at about nine years, which can confuse when assessing age.)

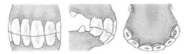

Eight years: From now on it is difficult to age the horse. But the shape and markings of the **incisor tables** can help (see Tooth tables, opposite).

Nine years: From the age of eight to nine years, the horse is said to be "aged". **Dental star** appears on centrals at eight years. Tables of laterals become triangular at nine.

Ten years: A brown mark called **Galvayne's Groove** appears on the upper corner incisors. The groove grows downward. Dental star now in all the lower incisors.

Fifteen years: Galvayne's Groove reaches about halfway down corner teeth.

Twenty years: The Groove reaches all the way down, then begins to disappear from the top downward. The teeth are very sloping.

Twenty-five years: Galvayne's Groove will have disappeared from the top half. As the horse grows older, the gums recede and the teeth appear longer.

Care of teeth

All horses should have their teeth checked every six months. When they chew food, their teeth suffer a lot of wear. Sometimes the wear is uneven. The grinding process on the molar teeth often creates sharp edges.

Mouth problems

The inside of a horse's cheeks and his tongue can be rubbed sore, and develop ulcers. Chewing is then painful and difficult, which can lead to indigestion and weight loss.

Problem teeth

Different types of problem teeth can appear and may need to be removed. For example, small teeth called **wolf teeth** can grow next to the first upper molar. They can be uncomfortable and interfere with the *bit**.
• A symptom of sharp teeth is when partly-chewed food falls from the horse's mouth while eating.

A solution to this problem is **floating**, which involves smoothing all the sharp edges of the molars. As these are at the back, they can be difficult to reach. A device called a **gag** is used to hold the jaws open for floating.

A horse having his incisor teeth checked for any problems

*Bits, 40

Horse colors

The hair covering a horse's skin lie at an angle and overlap to give protection against light wind and rain. The length and color of the hair depends on the breed of the horse or pony.

Coat colors

Horses and ponies are described according to the color of their hair. There are several main colors, such as black, brown, chestnut and gray, and there are also mixtures of these which are given different color descriptions.

Bay

Bay ranges from a red-brown color to a gold shade that is almost chestnut.
Bays always have black manes and tails, and the lower legs are also usually black.

Black

Black hair covers the whole body, including legs, mane, tail. Sometimes have white *markings**. A horse with a pure black summer coat and brown-black winter coat may be called a **summer back**.

Gray

Gray describes black skin with mixed black and white hairs. The coat grows lighter, until almost completely white.

Brown

Brown describes a mixture of black and brown color in the coat, with black limbs, mane and tail. Darker than a dark bay.

Chestnut

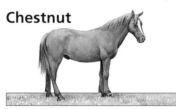

Chestnut covers various shades of gold-colored hair. The mane and tail should be the same color, but can be lighter or darker than the rest.
• **Light chestnuts** have more yellow in their manes and tails.

Blue dun

A **blue dun** is blue-black all over with a black skin beneath. There may be a *dorsal stripe** along the back, and black legs. It has a black mane and tail.

Yellow dun

The hair of a **yellow dun** is a strong yellow color. There may be a dorsal stripe and **zebra marks**, or stripes, on the legs. It often has black on the head and muzzle.

Palomino

Palomino is a gold color, with white mane and tail.

Spotted

Spotted describes a fine white coat with a pink skin beneath. The body is covered with black or brown spots.

This is sometimes described as an Appaloosa color. But not all spotted horses are *Appaloosas**, which have their own special coloring.

Strawberry roan

Strawberry roan describes a chestnut body color with a mixture of white hairs, giving a pink effect.

*Appaloosa, 29; Dorsal stripe, 25; Markings, 24

For a link to a website where you can look at lots of photographs of different horses, go to **www.usborne-quicklinks.com**

Blue roan

In a **blue roan**, the body color is black mixed with some white hair giving a blue-gray effect. The lower legs have black hair, sometimes with white markings.

Bay-brown

A **bay-brown** has the main color of brown, with a bay muzzle and black legs, tail and mane.

Black-brown

The main color in **black-brown** is black, but with a brown muzzle, and sometimes brown flanks.

Cream (or Cremello)

Cream describes a cream-colored coat and pink skin. The iris of the eye has little or no color, making the eye look pink or blue.

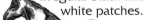

Piebald

A **piebald** coat has large, irregular black and white patches.

Skewbald

A **skewbald** has patches of white and any other color except black.

Pinto

Pinto is the term used in the USA to describe pie- or skewbald. Two types: Overo and Tobiano.

Albino

An **albino** has very light coloring. The pinky skin is covered with silky, snow-white coat, mane and tail. The eyes look pink.

Odd-colored

Odd-colored coats have large, irregular patches of more than two colors.

Whole-colored

Whole-colored are coats all of one color with no other color anywhere.

Types of hair

On some parts of the body, such as the nostrils and eyelids, the hair is very fine. On other parts, longer and stronger hair serves particular purposes.

• The hair on the tail and mane is very long and tough and is used to keep away insects and protect against weather. Long, thick eyelashes protect the eyes from dust and insects.

• In some places, such as on the chest and forehead, the hair comes together at different angles. These small areas are called **whorls**.

Hairs in ears keep out insects.

Whorl

Whiskers on muzzle act as "feelers".

23

Markings

The heads and legs of horses and ponies often have patches of white hair on them. These are called **markings**. The skin under the markings is also light-colored. Sometimes patches of white hair are caused by pressure from the saddle or harness, or damage to the skin. But in these cases, the skin beneath the patches is the same color as the rest of the skin.

Head markings

White markings on the head are given different names depending on their shape and size.

• A **snip** is a bright white spot on the top lip near the nostrils. The size and position of the snip is usually described.

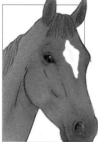

• A **star** is any white mark on the forehead. It can vary in shape and size.

• A **stripe** is a narrow white mark down the length of the face, from the eyes to the muzzle. It may or may not be attached to a star.

• A **blaze** is a white mark down the face to the muzzle. Described as **narrow**, **broad**, **irregular**, **broken** or **full**, depending on shape and size.

• A **white face**, or **bald face**, is a broad mark over the forehead and face, eyes, nose, and part of the muzzle.

• A **wall eye** is one which shows white or blue-white coloring in the iris instead of the normal coloring.

It is also known as **china eye** or **blue eye**, or sometimes **glass eye**. It does not indicate blindness.

Leg markings

White markings on the legs of a horse or pony are named according to the part of the leg they cover, and the upper limit of the marking.

• **Ermine marks** are small black or brown spots, which surround the *coronet** and occur on white leg markings. They look like ermine fur.

• A **white pastern** is a marking which runs around the pastern. Extends from the coronet, up the leg to the *fetlock joint**.

• A **sock** is a white marking extending from the coronet up the leg to above the fetlock joint. It should not normally extend up to the horse's knee joint or *hock**.

• A **stocking** is another type of white marking on the horse's leg. It should extend from the horse's knee or hock at the top, all the way down the leg to meet the foot.

*Coronet, 10; Fetlock joint, 10; Hock, 10

A dorsal stripe on a horse's back

Back markings

A **dorsal stripe**, or **eel stripe**, is a dark stripe - black, brown or dun - from the line of the neck along the back to the tail. It is often seen in *duns** and in North European and Asian breeds.

Hooves

The colors of hooves also vary and can act as good identification marks.

• **Dark horn** is a very dark brown, or black.

• **Pale horn** is a light, pale cream or honey color.

• **Mixed horn** is a mixture of both dark horn and pale horn.

Artificial markings

Markings can also be applied artificially to horses and ponies by their owners. There are a number of different types of artificial markings. They are all used as identification marks to distinguish horses belonging to different owners, and as deterrents against theft.

Brands

Brands usually indicate the stud, breed and/or country of origin of the horse or pony.

They are made with a red-hot branding iron, and placed on the shoulder, hindquarters, neck or hoof. Hoof brands indicate owner.

Freeze-branding

Freeze-branding is a modern way of branding by applying a super-chilled marker to a clipped area.

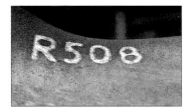

The mark is usually placed under the saddle, but it can also be placed on the shoulders or the neck.

The horse is freeze-branded with a serial number which is kept on a national register.

The serial number can be given to the police if the horse is stolen.

Tattoos

In North America, the inside of a horse's top lip is sometimes **tattooed**. Sometimes the tattoo is applied on the horse's ear.

This prevents the substitution of horses in races which have big prizes.

Some animals can suffer permanent nerve damage when they are given lip or ear tattoos.

Microchipping

Microchipping involves inserting a tiny electronic device called a silicon chip just beneath the horse's skin. It is usually done by a vet.

Microchipping is more useful as a means of locating a horse that has been stolen, rather than as a deterrent against theft.

A silicon chip is a tiny electric circuit board.

Breeds of the world

There are three main types of horses: ponies, horses and heavy horses. They all belong to the same species *Equus caballus**, but they are divided up into many different groups, or **breeds**, within the species. Horses are usually taller than ponies, and there are differences in build that distinguish horses and ponies from each other.

Ponies

Shetland
• **Height:** No more than 42in (106.6cm).
• **Color:** Any color, but not spotted. Dark brown and black are the most common.
• **Origin:** Scotland, Shetland and Orkney islands.
A very ancient breed, and the smallest of all Britain's eight native pony breeds. It is considered the strongest of all breeds for size.

New Forest
• **Height:** 12.2-14.2 *h.h.**
• **Color:** Any color except piebald, skewbald or blue-eyed cream.
• **Origin:** England: New Forest area.
Over 900 years, this breed has been mixed with other breeds. It is friendly and makes a good family pony.

Dartmoor
• **Height:** Up to 12.2 h.h.
• **Color:** Black, bay and brown with some *markings**.
• **Origin:** England: Dartmoor.
An ancient breed which has lived in southwest England for thousands of years. It makes an ideal first pony for a child, being small, narrow, and sensible, with a kind and gentle nature.

Exmoor
• **Height:** 11.2-12.3 h.h.
• **Color:** Bay, brown, dun. No white.

• **Origin:** England: moors of Somerset and Devon.
The oldest of the British native breeds, thought to have existed since prehistoric times. It is tough and makes a good riding pony, though it can be strong-willed.

Dale
• **Height:** 14-14.2 h.h.
• **Color:** Black, dark brown, bay or gray.
• **Origin:** England: north country Dales.
The Dale dates back to pre-Roman times. It can pull heavy loads and makes a good harness pony.

Fell
• **Height:** 13-14 h.h.
• **Color:** Black, bay, brown, sometimes gray.

• **Origin:** England: Westmorland/Cumberland. Related to the Dale, it is very strong and makes a good trekking pony.

Highland
• **Height:** 12.2-14.2 h.h.
• **Color:** Gray, black, brown and shades of dun.
• **Origin:** Scotland: Highlands. Two types - the larger **Mainland**, and the smaller **Island** type. Good for general riding.

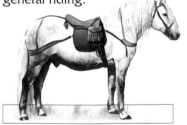

*Equus caballus, 4; h.h., 14; Markings, 24

For a link to a website where you can discover more details about different pony breeds, go to **www.usborne-quicklinks.com**

Welsh Mountain Pony (Section A)

- **Height:** Up to 12 h.h.
- **Color:** Any color (except piebald and skewbald), but gray is the most common color found.
- **Origin:** Wales.

One of the most common and also one of the most beautiful and popular of the native pony breeds. It has lived in the mountains and moorlands of Wales since Roman times. It is very intelligent and brave, as well as being kind and gentle. It is good as a child's riding pony and for harness work.

Welsh Pony (Section B)

- **Height:** Up to 13.2 h.h.
- **Color:** Any color except piebald and skewbald.
- **Origin:** Wales.

Developed from the Welsh Mountain Pony. It was used for shepherding on the hills of Wales, but is now mainly bred as a child's riding pony. Brave and intelligent with a strong character, it is the main riding pony of the Welsh breeds.

Welsh Pony, Cob Type (Section C)

- **Height:** Up to 13.2 h.h.
- **Color:** Any color except piebald and skewbald.
- **Origin:** Wales.

Developed from the Welsh Mountain Pony. Originally used for general farm work. Good in harness.

Connemara

- **Height:** 13-14.2 h.h.
- **Color:** Gray, bay, black, dun, chestnut, roan.

- **Origin:** Ireland: Connemara. Ireland's only native breed of pony, the Connemara is now also bred in other countries. It has good jumping ability. A good child's pony.

Haflinger

- **Height:** 13.1-14.2 h.h.
- **Color:** Palomino or chestnut, flaxen mane/tail.
- **Origin:** Austria: Tyrol region. A small, strong mountain breed. Good for draft (pulling) work and riding.

Fjord

- **Height:** 13-14 h.h.
- **Color:** An ancient breed with the characteristic dun coloring, *dorsal stripe** down the back and *zebra marks** on the legs.

- **Origin:** Norway.
The Fjord was used by the Vikings, and has spread into Germany as well as throughout Scandinavia. It is gentle and very strong, and is still used for farm work in some mountain areas.

Icelandic

- **Height:** 12-13.1 h.h.
- **Color:** Usually gray or dun, though all other colors may be seen.

- **Origin:** Iceland.
The only breed which has been bred pure, without any outside blood, for almost 1,000 years. Very hardy and tough. It shows a gait called the **tölt**, which is an unusual four-beat, very fast running walk. It is one of the toughest pony breeds, very intelligent and long-lived. It has excellent eyesight.

Breeds of the world

Horses

Akhal-Teke
- **Height:** Average 14.2-15.2 h.h.
- **Color:** Golden dun, bay, chestnut, gray, black.

- **Origin:** Central Asia: Turkoman Steppes.
A small, wiry horse with fine skin and silky hair. Descended from the ancient Turkmene or Turkoman horse, which goes back more than 2,500 years. It has incredible stamina and rides well in desert conditions. It can be bad-tempered.

Cleveland Bay
- **Height:** 15.2-16.2 h.h.
- **Color:** Bay or bay-brown.
- **Origin:** England: northern counties.
One of the oldest English breeds, it has been relatively free from outside influence. Large and well-made, it can be ridden, driven or used for light draft (pulling) work. A natural jumper and, crossed with the *Thoroughbred**, will produce a first class hunter, show jumper or carriage horse.

Hackney
- **Height:** Average just over 15 h.h.
- **Color:** Usually bay, brown, black, chestnut.
- **Origin:** England.
A descendant of the old Norfolk Roadster, a famous breed of trotting horse bred in the 18th century. Elegant, with a pretty face. Lively and full of character, the Hackney has both Arab and Thoroughbred blood in its veins. Famous for its high, springing trot, which is spectacular and very showy.

Arab
- **Height:** Average 14-15 h.h.
- **Color:** Gray, chestnut, bay, occasionally black.
- **Origin:** Arabian Peninsula.
The most famous horse of all, celebrated throughout history for its beauty and elegance. The oldest and purest breed in existence today, the desert Arabian has been bred for over 1,000 years, first by the Bedouin in the Arabian Peninsula, and later in Europe. It combines all the best qualities, being brave, gentle, tough and intelligent.

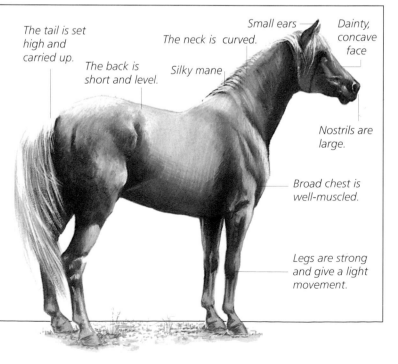

The tail is set high and carried up.

The back is short and level.

The neck is curved.

Silky mane

Small ears

Dainty, concave face

Nostrils are large.

Broad chest is well-muscled.

Legs are strong and give a light movement.

For a link to a website where you can watch a video clip about Przewalski's horses, go to **www.usborne-quicklinks.com**

Scale
There is a very wide range of sizes between the different breeds of horse.

Falabella   Przewalski   Arab   American Saddlebred   Hanoverian

American Saddlebred
- **Height:** Average 15-16 h.h.
- **Color:** Bay, brown, black, chestnut.

- **Origin:** U.S.A.: Kentucky. This breed was developed by plantation owners of Kentucky during the 19th century. Today it is bred mainly for the show ring.

Appaloosa
- **Height:** Up to 15.2 h.h.
- **Color:** Five main color patterns, described as: frost, leopard-spotted, marble, snowflake, spotted blanket.

- **Origin:** U.S.A.: Idaho. One of the most popular U.S. breeds. It was bred by the Nez Perce Indians, and is descended from horses brought by Spanish settlers.

Andalusian
- **Height:** 15.2 h.h.
- **Color:** Gray, black, sometimes dun and palomino.
- **Origin:** Spain: Andalusia. Intelligent and affectionate, a breed celebrated throughout the world, it was the most famous horse in Europe until the emergence of the Thoroughbred in the 18th century. Descended from horses taken to Spain by the Moors from North Africa.

Camargue
- **Height:** Up to 15 h.h.
- **Color:** Gray. Foals born black, dark gray or brown, but their coats lighten with age.

- **Origin:** France: Camargue region.
Known as the "white horse of the sea". The white coat is the most striking feature. It thrives on the tough grass of the salt marshes.
Conformation * is usually poor. Has a high-stepping walk and is good at turning.

Przewalski's Horse
- **Height:** 12-14 h.h.
- **Color:** Dun with *dorsal stripe* * and leg stripes.
- **Origin:** Mongolia.
A wild horse discovered in 1881 by Russian explorer Colonel N.M. Przewalski. It is the last truly wild horse or pony. It is thought to be one of the basic breeds from which all horses have evolved. In the wild it was hunted almost to extinction, although a number are now being bred in zoos around the world. In its wild state, the Przewalski is powerfully built. It has many distinctive wild features: its dun color, an upright mane, the dorsal stripe on its back and *zebra markings* *.

*Conformation, 16; Dorsal stripe, 25; Zebra marks, 22

Breeds of the world

Horses

Morgan
- **Height:** Up to 15.2 h.h.
- **Color:** Usually bay, chestnut, brown, black.
- **Origin:** U.S.A.

Goes back to the 18th century and probably has *Arab* * and Thoroughbred blood. Modern Morgans are taller and more elegant than the originals. It is a good all-arounder, and as a carriage horse and a riding horse.

Lusitano
- **Height:** 15-16 h.h.
- **Color:** Usually gray.
- **Origin:** Portugal.

This horse looks very like the *Andalusian* *. It is probably of basic Andalusian stock with some Arab blood added. It is a good-looking, compact horse. Intelligent, agile and brave, it was orginally bred as a *cavalry* * horse. Today it is used in the bullring, where its agility is displayed.

Dutch Warmblood
- **Height:** 15.2-16.2 h.h.
- **Color:** Chestnut, gray, bay, and black/dark brown.
- **Origin:** Holland.

Two types: Gelderland and Groningen. The Gelderland of southern Holland is famous as a harness horse and a *show jumper* *. The heavier Groningen from northern Holland is used in farming and as a riding horse.

Quarter Horse
- **Height:** 15.2-16.1 h.h.
- **Color:** Any solid color, mainly chestnut.
- **Origin:** U.S.A.

An attractive horse, and North America's most popular breed. Developed by the early English colonists, by crossing mares of Spanish descent with imported English stallions. Its name comes from the quarter-mile sprints raced by the settlers down the streets of towns.

Hanoverian
- **Height:** 16-17 h.h.
- **Color:** All solid colors.
- **Origin:** Germany: Hanover.

The most important and one of the oldest of the German *warm blood* * breeds, the Hanoverian traces its descent back to the 18th century.

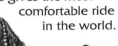

The modern horse has Thoroughbred blood, to give more courage and stamina.

Tennessee Walking Horse
- **Height:** 15-16 h.h.
- **Color:** Bay, black or chestnut.
- **Origin:** U.S.A.

Another popular breed from North America. A particular characteristic is a unique running walk. This is a very comfortable pace for the rider and some people claim that the horse gives the most comfortable ride in the world.

*Andalusian, 29; Arab, 28; Cavalry, 7; Show jumping, 76; Warm blood, 5

For a link to a website where you can follow an illustrated history of the beautiful Lusitano horse, go to **www.usborne-quicklinks.com**

Falabella

- **Height:** Does not exceed 76cm (30ins).
- **Color:** All colors.
- **Origin:** Argentina: Buenos Aires province.

The smallest horse in the world. Although very small, the Falabella is really a miniature horse rather than a pony. It was bred by the Falabella family near **Buenos Aires**, by crossing a small Thoroughbred horse with small *Shetland ponies**, and then inbreeding. Although it is strong, the horse is more suitable as a pet than as a saddle horse.

Full-grown Falabella beside a full-grown person

Thoroughbred

- **Height:** Average 16.1 h.h.
- **Color:** Usually brown, bay and chestnut.
- **Origin:** England.

The fastest and most famous racehorse in the world. It is also one of the most beautiful of all horses.

The breed was developed in the 17th and 18th centuries in England by crossing Arab stallions with native mares. It is now also used in show jumping, *horse trials** and *dressage**. It makes an excellent hunter.

Apart from its own ancestor, the Arab, the Thoroughbred has had more influence on other breeds than any horse. It has been used to establish new breeds and improve others throughout the world.

Lipizzaner

- **Height:** Average 15-15.2 h.h.
- **Color:** Main color is gray.
- **Origin:** Austria: Lipizza.

Well-known for its obedience and intelligence, this breed is famous for its connection with the *Spanish Riding School** of Vienna. It has been bred since the 16th century, with the foundation stud at Lipizza. The original Lipizza stock was pure Andalusian from Spain.

It is a compact, good-looking horse with a strong back and quarters and short, strong legs. Most horses are gray. Foals are born black or brown and can take up to 10 years to acquire their gray coats. Famous for its *high school** work, it also makes a good *driving** horse.

Trakehner

- **Height:** 16-16.2 h.h.
- **Color:** Any solid color, though usually chestnut, bay or black.

- **Origin:** Germany: East Prussia.

One of the most famous horses in military history, known for its great endurance. Originally bred at the stud at Trakehnen in East Prussia, founded in 1732. Schwerken horses of East Prussia were crossed with Polish Arabs. A lightweight type was bred to be ridden, while a heavier horse was used to pull guns. Today it is bred privately and is a top-class saddle horse with good *conformation**, and makes a good jumper. It is a handsome horse, with an elegant neck and good eyes.

*Conformation, 16; Dressage, 74; Driving, 92; High school, 99; Horse trials, 78; Shetland pony, 26; Spanish Riding School, 98

Breeds of the world

Heavy horses

Clydesdale
- **Height:** Average 16.2 h.h.
- **Color:** Bay, brown, sometimes gray and black.
- **Origin:** Scotland: Lanarkshire.

A heavy horse originating in the Clyde Valley, Lanarkshire in Scotland. In the mid-18th century, the local mares were crossed with much heavier Flemish stallions. It is not as big as the Shire but, like that horse, it has been exported to countries requiring good draft (pulling) horses.

Irish Draft
- **Height:** 15-17 h.h.
- **Color:** Gray, bay, brown and chestnut.
- **Origin:** Ireland.

A light draft horse, it is an excellent farm worker, being quiet, intelligent and sensible. It was bred for the farm and also for riding. Its main use today is in producing top class *hunters** and *show jumpers** when crossed with *Thoroughbred** stallions or other high quality lightweight horses.

Suffolk Punch
- **Height:** 16-16.2 h.h.
- **Color:** Always described as "chesnut", without a t.
- **Origin:** England: Suffolk.

A heavy draft horse originating in the second half of the 18th century. It is one of the purest of all breeds of heavy horse, and is kind and intelligent. The modern Suffolk is a compact but wide horse, with short, powerful legs.

Percheron
- **Height:** 15.2-17 h.h.
- **Color:** Gray or black.
- **Origin:** France: La Perche region.

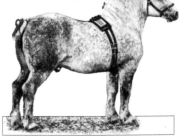

The Percheron is a rugged, active horse, intelligent and easy to handle. It has *Arab** blood in it, and is an elegant and well-proportioned animal. It is now exported to many parts of the world. It is the most popular carthorse in the world.

Shire
- **Height:** Up to 18 h.h., sometimes more
- **Color:** Bay, brown, black or gray.
- **Origin:** England: central counties known as shires.

One of the largest horses in the world, the Shire is a descendant of the Old English Black Horse, which is descended from the Great Horse of medieval times. Extremely strong, big-barreled and weighing about 1.016 tonne (1 ton).

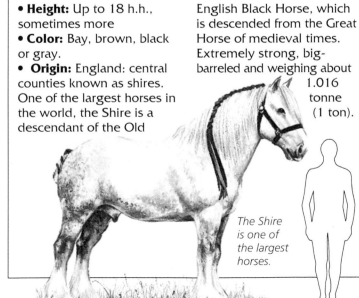

The Shire is one of the largest horses.

*Arab, 28; Hunters, 82; Show jumping, 76; Thoroughbred, 31

For a link to a website where you can find out more about heavy breeds, go to **www.usborne-quicklinks.com**

Ardennais

- **Height:** Up to 15.3 h.h.
- **Color:** Usually bay, roan, chestnut or gray.
- **Origin:** France/Belgium: Ardennes region.

A stocky, compact, powerful draft horse on short legs with very big bones. The extreme climate of the Ardennes region produces very strong horses of medium height, which are well-suited to farm work.

Breton

- **Height:** Up to 16 h.h.
- **Color:** Usually chestnut, sometimes black, bay or roan.
- **Origin:** France: Brittany.

The Draft Breton is a Breton with infusions of Percheron, Ardennais and Boulonnais blood. It has a powerful body with short legs, is an active horse with a kind nature and makes a good work horse.

Distribution of the breeds

The map below shows the areas where different breeds of ponies and horses originated. Western Europe has been enlarged as most of the breeds came from there.

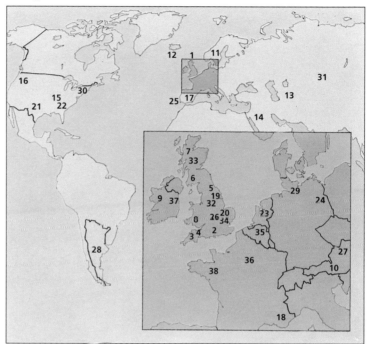

1	Shetland	20	Hackney
2	New Forest	21	Quarter Horse
3	Dartmoor	22	Tennessee Walking Horse
4	Exmoor	23	Dutch Warmblood
5	Dale	24	Trakehner
6	Fell	25	Lusitano
7	Highland	26	Thoroughbred
8	Welsh Mountain	27	Lipizzaner
9	Connemara	28	Falabella
10	Haflinger	29	Hanoverian
11	Fjord	30	Morgan
12	Icelandic	31	Przewalski's horse
13	Akhal-Teke	32	Shire
14	Arab	33	Clydesdale
15	American Saddlebred	34	Suffolk Punch
16	Appaloosa	35	Ardennais
17	Andalusian	36	Percheron
18	Camargue	37	Irish Draft
19	Cleveland Bay	38	Breton

33

 # Saddlery

Saddlery is often referred to as **tack**. It consists of a saddle with its fittings (girth, stirrup leathers and stirrup irons), and a bridle and its bit. There are many types of saddles and accessories to suit different horses and ponies, and different types of riding.

Points of the saddle

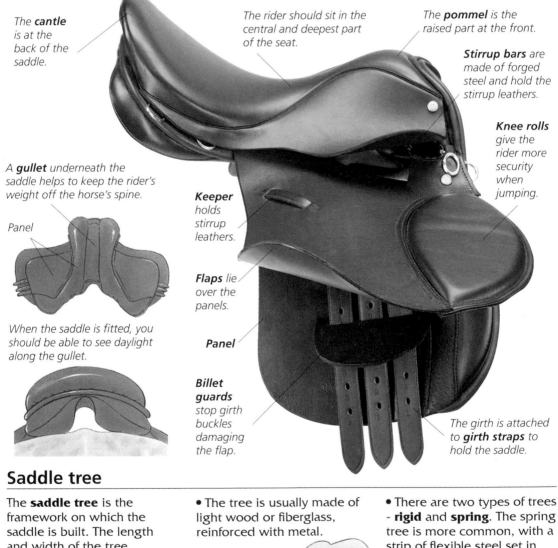

The **cantle** is at the back of the saddle.

The rider should sit in the central and deepest part of the seat.

The **pommel** is the raised part at the front.

Stirrup bars are made of forged steel and hold the stirrup leathers.

Knee rolls give the rider more security when jumping.

A **gullet** underneath the saddle helps to keep the rider's weight off the horse's spine.

Panel

When the saddle is fitted, you should be able to see daylight along the gullet.

Keeper holds stirrup leathers.

Flaps lie over the panels.

Panel

Billet guards stop girth buckles damaging the flap.

The girth is attached to **girth straps** to hold the saddle.

Saddle tree

The **saddle tree** is the framework on which the saddle is built. The length and width of the tree determines the length and width of the saddle. The saddle has to fit the horse, or it will be uncomfortable.

- The tree is usually made of light wood or fiberglass, reinforced with metal.

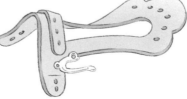

- There are two types of trees - **rigid** and **spring**. The spring tree is more common, with a strip of flexible steel set in both sides. This type is more comfortable for the rider and it is easier for the horse to feel the rider's *seat aids**.

34   *Seat aids, 68

For a link to a website where you can see pictures of lots of different types of saddles, go to **www.usborne-quicklinks.com**

Types of saddles

A saddle spreads the rider's weight evenly over the muscles of the horse's back, and helps the rider to sit in the correct position. Saddles vary in shape according to their different uses, such as jumping, hunting, dressage, showing or racing.

• The **general purpose saddle** is for all-purpose riding, such as *training**, and *hacking**. It often has a slightly flatter seat, and a forward cut which makes it suitable for many uses.

• A **showing saddle** has straighter flaps and fits closely on the horse's back. It is designed to show an unbroken back line to judges and to show off the horse's front.

• The **jumping saddle** has flaps cut farther forward, enabling the rider to use shorter-length stirrups. Shorter stirrups allow the rider to keep his or her balance over the jumps.

• The seat of a **dressage saddle** is slightly dipped to allow the rider to sit deeply in the center. Long stirrup leathers and straight flaps allow the rider close contact with the whole of the leg.

• The **endurance saddle** is designed to spread the rider's weight as much as possible over the horse's back. This is comfortable for long *endurance rides**.

• The **racing saddle** is made of the lightest materials. The seat is not so important and the rider keeps in contact with the horse by means of the leathers and stirrup irons.

• **Pad saddles** are designed for small children. They have either no tree, or just a tree forepart. A pad saddle usually has its own webbing girth permanently attached to it, and often has a handle on the front.

• The **Western saddle** is used for *Western riding**. It is heavier than most saddles but is designed to fit the horse's back comfortably. It is fitted with a pad or blanket.

Additional tack

• The **breastplate** is a leather neck strap attached to the front of the saddle to stop the saddle from slipping back.

• A **crupper** is a leather strap with a loop at one end which fits under the horse's tail. It prevents a saddle or *roller** slipping forward.

Crupper

Breastplate

Saddle pad

• A **saddle pad** is a pad cut in the shape of a saddle and worn under the saddle to protect a horse's back, and the underside of the saddle.
• Cotton is the best material as it is cheap, absorbs sweat and is easy to clean.
• Sheepskin is good, though it is also the most expensive material.
• Felt is good, but expensive and can be difficult to clean.

Endurance rides, 86; Hacking, 66; Roller, 42; Training, 62; Western riding, 72   35

 # Saddlery

Girths

A **girth** secures a saddle on a horse's back. Girths are very important, both for the safety of the rider and the comfort of the horse. They should not rub or slip. They are usually made from materials such as leather, webbing, nylon and lampwick.

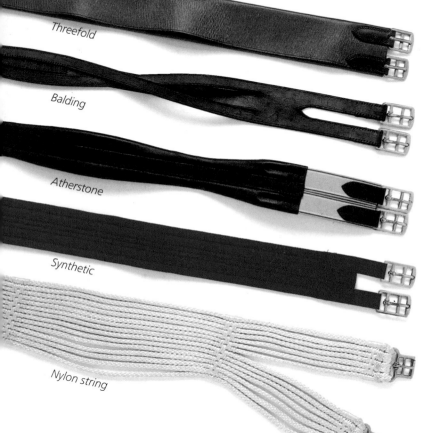

Threefold

Balding

Atherstone

Synthetic

Nylon string

• A **threefold girth** is made from one piece of leather, folded to form three layers with two buckles at each end.

• A **balding girth** is a leather girth with two buckles at each end. The middle part is divided into three separate straps and crossed over. This design reduces the width behind the horse's elbows and is less likely to rub or pinch him.

• An **atherstone girth** consists of a piece of soft leather which is folded and shaped at the elbows, like a balding girth. This design helps to reduce the chance of *galls** or saddle sores.

• A **synthetic girth** has a soft filling, designed for comfort and strength. Some synthetic girths have the same shape as an atherstone girth.

• A **nylon string girth** is made of nylon strands, which are stitched together at intervals. It makes a good, general-purpose girth which is strong and gives a good grip around the horse. But it can pinch the horse if it is not carefully fitted.

Putting on a saddle

The saddle enables the rider to sit comfortably and correctly on the horse. But the horse must also feel comfortable.

• The seat of the saddle should be level on the horse's back and must not be too long. The saddle must not slip when the horse moves or it will rub him.

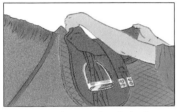

Run the stirrups up. Lift the saddle onto the *withers** and slide back into position.

Fasten the girth so that it is firm but not tight. You will need to tighten it again later.

36   *Galls, 59; Withers, 10

For a link to a website where you can study step-by-step instructions and pictures that show you how to put on a saddle, go to **www.usborne-quicklinks.com**

Stirrup irons

Stirrup irons should be made of stainless steel and allow about 1cm (½in) on each side of the rider's foot. Children must not use full-size adult stirrup irons as their feet can slip through.

Safety stirrups

Safety stirrups are designed to prevent the rider's foot from becoming wedged in the stirrup. Rubber treads are often used to prevent the foot from slipping.

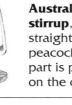

• The **peacock safety stirrup** is designed for children. It has a thick rubber ring on the outside instead of metal. This pulls off if the foot is pulled out of the stirrup. This design does not hang straight, as it weighs more on one side than the other. Sometimes it bends when under pressure.

• The **bent leg**, or **Australian safety stirrup**, hangs straighter than the peacock. The bent part is positioned on the outside.

Stirrup leathers

Stirrup leathers attach the stirrups to the saddle. When new, they will stretch a little. To ensure that this stretching is even, the leathers should be changed around regularly.

• The best quality oak bark-tanned **leather** is the nicest and most suitable for normal riding.

• **Rawhide** is very strong and the best leather for *cross-country riding**.

• **Buffalo hide** is also extremely strong. This type often stretches more than other types, but it is almost unbreakable.

Tack care

Saddlery is expensive, but if it is looked after properly it should last a long time. If it is not properly cared for, leather can become dry and crack or break. It needs to be regularly treated with special dressings such as vegetable or animal oils.

Carrying the saddle

To prevent damage and to leave a hand free for opening doors, a saddle should be carried in one of two ways.

• With the front arch in the crook of your elbow.

• Against your side, with the hand in the front arch.

Cleaning

Put the saddle on a wooden stand called a **saddle stand**. Then remove the girth and billet guards, stirrup leathers and the stirrup irons.

• Use a damp cloth to remove all dirt and grease. Use a chamois-leather or cloth to remove moisture.

• Rub in saddle-soap with a damp sponge, using a circular motion. If the soap lathers, it means the sponge is too wet. The leather will get hard when it dries and will eventually crack.

• The seat, panel flaps and girth straps should all be thoroughly cleaned in the same way.

• The stirrup leathers, leather girths and leather bridles should also be cleaned in the same way.

• All the metalwork - the bits, stirrup irons, buckles, rings, and all the other pieces - should be cleaned with water, and then thoroughly dried and polished with a soft cloth.

Bridles

The **bridle** is the headgear for a horse. It consists of straps with buckles, and a metal mouthpiece, called a *bit**, which is used to control the animal through the reins. Bridles come in three sizes - pony, cob and full - and various widths. It is important to use the one that suits the job and horse's head.

Snaffle bridle

The **snaffle bridle** is the simplest and most common, with headpiece, throat latch, browband and cheekpieces.

*The **headpiece**, together with the cheekpieces, keeps the bit in the horse's mouth.*

Brow band

Throat latch *helps to keep the bridle in position.*

Cheekpieces *are attached to the bit and the headpiece.*

Noseband (see page opposite) fits around the nose and above the bit.

The bit goes in the mouth to help control and direct the horse. Different types can be used.

Double bridle

The **double bridle** is used for *showing** and *dressage**. It has two bits: a small type of *snaffle bit**, called a **bridoon**, and a *weymouth**, or curb bit. This bridle is the same as the snaffle bridle, but it has an extra strap called a **sliphead** to hold the snaffle bit.

Cheekpiece

Noseband

Bridoon

Curb chain

Weymouth

• The weymouth is held by the headpiece and cheekpieces. The bridoon is held by the sliphead.
• The weymouth is used with a *curb chain** and *lip strap **, with a sliding or fixed mouthpiece. A bridoon is a type of snaffle bit, but lighter, with a thinner mouthpiece. Like the snaffle bit, it raises the head, while the weymouth serves to position the horse's nose.

Lip strap

Bitless bridle

The **bitless bridle** (or **hackamore**) has no mouthpiece. It acts by putting pressure on the nose, lower jaw and *poll**, but not on the mouth. The reins are attached to long cheekpieces which act like levers on the special noseband. They press against the top of the nose and lower jaw, giving the rider control over the animal. Bitless bridles must not be fitted too low as they can interfere with the horse's breathing.

• The **scawbrig** is the simplest and mildest of all the bitless bridles. It can be very useful for horses with mouth or bit problems. It can

be used by beginners, unlike some of the more severe types of bitless bridles. Because of its mildness, it can be used for reschooling difficult horses and ponies.
• The **Blair's pattern** design of bitless bridle is much more severe than the scawbrig. The metal shanks can exert a very strong pressure on the nose and jaw. So this should be used only by skilled riders. The noseband should be padded to stop any rubbing.

38

*Bits, 40; Curb chain, 41; Dressage, 74; Lip strap, 41; Poll, 10; Showing, 82; Snaffle bit, 40; Weymouth, 40

For a link to a website where you can test your knowledge of the terms used for parts of a bridle, go to
www.usborne-quicklinks.com

- The **continental hackamore**, also called a **jumping hackamore**, is another form of a mild and simple bitless bridle.
- The **bosal** is a type of bitless bridle which is sometimes used in *Western riding**. It acts on the nose and jaw and is usually made of braided rawhide. It must be carefully fitted to prevent any rubbing around the horse's jaw.

Reins

Reins are made in different widths to suit the size of the rider's hands. They are attached to the *cheek rings** of the bit.
- A double bridle uses two pairs of reins; a snaffle bridle only one pair. One rein on a double bridle is wider than the other so the rider can distinguish between them.
- **Plain leather reins** give the best feel for the rider. But they can become slippery in rain, or on a sweaty horse.

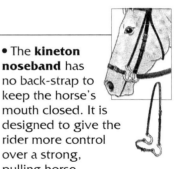

Rubber

Plain leather

Laced

- **Laced leather reins** are less slippery, but they are expensive and hard to clean.
- **Rubber-covered reins** give the best grip in rain, or on a pulling or sweaty horse.
- **Leather grips** prevent the reins from slipping through the rider's hands.

Nosebands

A **noseband** is used to prevent a horse from avoiding the action of the bit, which reduces the rider's control. It is also used to give an attractive appearance to the head.

- The **cavesson** is the simplest type of noseband. It fits around the nose, above the bit, and inside the cheekpieces. It is the only type used with a double bridle and bits with curb chains.

- The **drop noseband** has a rear strap which is fastened below the bit. It should be fitted firmly to stop the horse from opening his mouth. You should be able to fit one finger between noseband and nose.

- The **figure-eight noseband** is used for the same purpose as the drop, but has an extra strap above the bit. It also acts over a wider area and prevents a horse from opening and/or crossing his jaw.

- The **flash noseband** is a cavesson noseband which fits more closely and with an extra lower strap on the front of the noseband. The strap should pass above the nostrils on the front of the nose.

- The **kineton noseband** has no back-strap to keep the horse's mouth closed. It is designed to give the rider more control over a strong, pulling horse.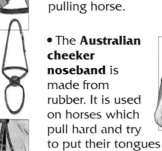

- The **Australian cheeker noseband** is made from rubber. It is used on horses which pull hard and try to put their tongues over the bit.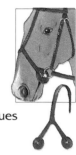

- The **sheepskin noseband** is similar to the cavesson. It is used on *racehorses**, to prevent them from shying and throwing up their heads. In the U.S.A. it is known as a **shadow roll**.

*Cheek rings, 40; Racing, 84; Western riding, 72   39

 # Bits

The **bit** is the part of the *bridle** that fits into the horse's mouth over the tongue. The bit acts on one or more parts of the horse's mouth and head: the lips and corners of the mouth; the tongue; the bars of the mouth; the roof of the mouth; the nose; the chin-groove; and the *poll**. It is controlled by the rider through the reins.

Types of bits

• The **jointed snaffle bit** is the most popular bit. Made of metal, rubber, nylon or synthetic material, it has one joint in the middle. It acts mainly on the lips and corners of the mouth, the bars of the mouth and also on the tongue.

Jointed snaffle

• The **pelham bit** combines a curb bit and a *bridoon**, so that it performs the job of two bits in one.

Pelham

• The **gag** is a type of snaffle bit. It acts on lips, corners of the mouth, the tongue and poll, and can be very severe.

• The **kimberwick bit** has a straight bar and small tongue-port (curved section). It is used with a curb chain, and is milder than a pelham.

• The **straight bar snaffle bit** acts on the lips, corners of mouth and the tongue. For horses with damaged or tender mouths or lips.

Straight bar snaffle

Dutch gag

• The **Doctor Bristol bit** is a type of double-jointed snaffle bit. Its central plate is rectangular and at an angle, and presses on the tongue. It is a fairly severe bit.

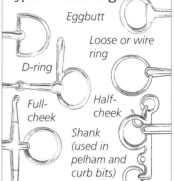

Cheek rings

Cheekpieces* attach the bridle headpiece to **cheek rings**. There are different types of cheek rings.

Eggbutt

Loose or wire ring

D-ring

Full-cheek

Half-cheek

Shank (used in pelham and curb bits)

• The **American gag** and **Dutch gag bits** are used to help control strong horses. Their effect is to raise the horse's head. The Dutch gag can be made milder or more severe according to which of the three small rings the reins are attached to. The lowest ring is the most severe.

• The **weymouth**, or **curb bit**, is used with a curb chain and lip strap. It acts mainly on the bars of the mouth, the tongue, poll, corners of the mouth and curb groove. The longer the arms of a bit, the more severe the action.

The correct way to fit a bit

When fitted, the bit should reach the corners of the horse's lips. It should not be too high or too low.

If it is fitted too high, the bit will pull up the corners of the horse's lips. This will cause him discomfort.

If too low, the bit will drop down and not be in contact with the lips. This reduces the rider's control.

*Bridle, 38; Bridoon, 38; Cheekpieces, 38; Poll, 10

For a link to a website where you can study a simple diagram that shows how a bit sits inside a horse's mouth, go to **www.usborne-quicklinks.com**

The mouthpiece

The **mouthpiece** is the part of the bit which rests in the horse's mouth. Wide diameter mouthpieces are milder than narrow ones, because they spread the pressure over a wider area.

Bars - the area of the mouth where the bit rests

- **Single-jointed mouthpieces** have a nutcracker action. They are quite mild and give better control than straight bar and mullen mouthpieces.

- **Double-jointed mouthpieces** are even milder as the nutcracker action is reduced.

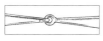

- **Straight bar mouthpieces** are on the simplest snaffle bits. A variation is the **mullen mouthpiece**. This has a slightly curved shape, which allows more room for the tongue. Both are mild.
- **Ports** are sometimes included. This is where the middle of the mouthpiece is slightly raised. This allows more room for the tongue, but increases pressure on the bars of the mouth.

- **Twisted mouthpieces** have a twisted bar. The ridges make this a severe type.
- Mouthpieces with **rollers** (below) are severe. Prevent horses from pulling and leaning on the bit.

Extra fittings

- **Bit guards** are flat rubber disks with holes in the middle. They are used to help prevent the corners of the mouth or the lips from being rubbed.

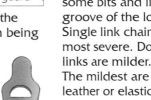
Bit guard

- Metal **tongue grids** or rubber **tongue ports** stop a horse from putting his tongue over the mouthpiece to avoid the rider's control.

Tongue port

Martingales

Martingales prevent the horse from raising his head too high. There are two main types: the standing martingale and the running martingale.

- The **running martingale** is divided into two at the chest. It is attached to the *girth** and passes between the forelegs. It is used on a horse which carries his head too high. Pressure is put on the mouth via the reins to lower the horse's head.

- The **standing martingale** is fitted at one end to the girth, and at the other to a *cavesson noseband**. It stops the horse from raising his head too high, and helps to prevent the horse from hitting the rider in the face with his head.

- **Curb chains** (above and right) are used on some bits and lie in the chin groove of the lower jaw. Single link chains are the most severe. Double or treble links are milder. The mildest are leather or elastic.

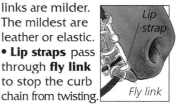
Fly link

- **Lip straps** pass through **fly link** to stop the curb chain from twisting.

Lip strap
Fly link

- The **Irish martingale** is the simplest type. It keeps the reins in place and prevents them from going over the horse's head.

- The **Market Harborough martingale** has two strong leather straps which pull the bit down as soon as the horse throws his head up.

Extra fittings

- **Rein stops** (below) prevent the reins from getting caught up on the bit rings.
- **Martingale stops** prevent the breaststrap catching up on the feet.

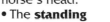
Rein stop

*Cavesson noseband, 39; Girths, 36

Horse and rider clothing

Bandages, sheets and blankets are all called **horse clothing**. Usually, a horse's own coat will keep him warm enough. But in winter months, or if he has been clipped or is sick, he will need clothing for extra warmth. Riders also wear special clothes.

Blankets

It is important that a blanket fits well. It might slip if too loose or rub if too tight. The blanket should lie straight and flat and cover the *withers** at the front and the *quarters** at the back. Blankets should be cleaned regularly, and aired as often as possible to keep them fresh and to prevent irritation.

- The **New Zealand blanket** is designed to protect against wind and rain. It was traditionally made from canvas lined with wool. Today it is normally made from synthetic materials.
- The **stable/night blanket** was also made of wool or jute, but is now made of synthetic materials.

Roller

Outer layer for protection

The lining of the stable blanket gives warmth.

- A **blanket liner** is a light wool or synthetic blanket which provides extra warmth under the night blanket.
- A wool **dress sheet** is used to replace the stable blanket when traveling or at *events**. It comes in bright colors.
- An **exercise sheet** is a short blanket which fits under the saddle. It provides extra warmth during exercise.

- An **anti-sweat sheet** is made of cotton mesh, and is worn under a light blanket. It is used in barns and helps a horse to cool off after exercise, without danger of catching cold. It is also used for traveling.
- A **cooler** is a large, square blanket made of light wool, cotton or synthetic materials. It is worn when drying off after exercise if sweaty, or after a bath. It cools off a horse in cold weather without chilling him.
- A **summer sheet** is used in summer instead of a blanket. Cotton or linen, it is shaped like a stable blanket and is used to keep a horse's coat clean before *showing**.
- A **rain sheet** is a waterproof exercise sheet which is used outdoors.
- A **neck hood** covers the whole neck and head. It helps to keep a horse clean, dry and warm outside.

Keeping blankets in place

Once a blanket is fitted, it must be securely fastened to stop it from slipping off. Rollers and straps help to keep it in place.

- The **roller** goes around a horse's belly and is used to keep blankets in place. It has two stuffed pads which lie on either side of the spine and raise the roller off the spine. This eases pressure to give a more comfortable fit.

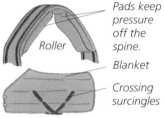

Pads keep pressure off the spine.

Roller

Blanket

Crossing surcingles

- A **surcingle** is the same as a roller, except that it has no built-in pads. A foam pad should therefore be placed beneath it.
- **Crossing surcingles** are better than rollers and surcingles as they place no pressure on the spine, and stop blankets from slipping.
- A **tail strap** passed around the hindquarters stops light blankets from blowing up.
- **Leg straps** keep blankets straight and prevent them from blowing up. The left one is secured around the left hind leg. The right strap threads through the left strap.

Events, 78; Quarters, 10; Showing, 82; Withers, 10

For a link to a website where you can find out more about horse clothing, go to **www.usborne-quicklinks.com**

Bandages

Leg bandages give the legs extra warmth and support. They can also be used to keep a *poultice** in place on an injured leg. They should never be put on too tightly or wet, and should always be kept clean.

• **Tail bandages** are put on after *grooming**, to lay the hairs in the horse's tail flat, and to keep the tail neat. They are also used to protect the tail when the horse is traveling.

• **Stable bandages** are wide leg bandages of thick wool or cotton, with some padding beneath. They go from below the knee down to the *coronet**. They are used to keep a horse warm. They also help to dry muddy legs after exercise and can be used for protection when traveling.

• **Exercise bandages** are made of crepe or elasticated fabric. They are applied from below the knee to above the *fetlock joint**. Cotton or synthetic pads are always placed underneath. They protect the legs against scratches when riding in rough country. They also help to absorb shock when jumping or galloping.

Clothing for traveling

• The **halter** is made of leather or cotton or nylon web. It is used to tie up a horse when it is being transported, groomed, or when it is being led.

• This **halter** is a simpler version. It is usually made of rope or cotton webbing, and is used for leading or tying up a horse.

• The **head bumper** is made of felt and leather, and protects the top of the head.

A horse for traveling. A warmer blanket is worn in winter.

• The **tail guard** is made of soft leather or cloth and is tied around the top of the tail. It prevents the tail from being rubbed while the horse is traveling in a trailer.

Quick-release knot

A **quick-release knot** can be quickly released by the handler in an emergency.

The lead rope is made into a loop, with its end across the rest.

Another loop is made in the free end. The second loop is pulled through the first.

Pull down on the second loop. To undo quickly, pull on the free end.

Head bumper

Halter

Surcingle

Summer sheet

Sweat sheet

Knee boots

Hock boots are made of thick leather and protect the hocks.

Stable bandages

Coronet, 10; Fetlock joint, 12; Grooming, 54; Poultice, 61   43

Horse and rider clothing

Horse's boots

There are various types of boots designed to prevent a horse from injuring himself or being injured while moving, especially when being schooled, jumping or galloping. The boots are made in a variety of materials and designs.

• The **galloping boot** is one of the most common. It is made of padded leather or felt, or synthetic material. It is for a horse that often brushes (hits) the inside of one leg with the inside edge of the opposite hoof.

Galloping boot

• The **fetlock boot** is a type of brushing boot. It protects the *fetlock joints** from brushing, if the horse moves close behind or in front.

• The **over-reach** or **bell boot** is used for jumping. It consists of a rubber bell shape which is fitted over the hoof. It is designed to

Over-reach boot

protect the heels of the horse's forelegs from being hit by the toe of a shoe on one of the hind feet.

• Both **knee** and **hock boots** are used for protection when traveling. *Hock** boots must be put on in the stable before the horse is put in the trailer.

Hock boot

• The **tendon boot** is designed to give extra protection to the leg *tendons**.

Tendon boot

• **Shipping boots** are also designed to prevent injury while the horse is being transported. Made of synthetic fiber, they cover the leg from above or just below the knee or hock, down to the *coronet**, which they overlap. They can be used as an alternative to *bandages**.

Traveling boots

• Padded **sausage boots** fit around the *pastern** to stop the heel of the shoe from hitting the elbow when the horse is lying down. They are only used if the horse has been injured, or if the shoe heels are very long.

Sausage boot

• The **fetlock** or **brushing ring** is a rubber anti-brushing ring which fits just above the fetlock joint on the leg. It keeps the opposite leg away.

Fetlock ring

• A **coronet boot** is worn to just above the line of the coronet. Made of leather and felt, it is designed to protect the coronet from any injuries.

Coronet boot

Rider's clothing

Correct clothes make riding safer and more comfortable. The clothes should help a rider to feel relaxed and should never prevent him or her from keeping in close contact with the horse or interfere with movement.

Hats

• A rider should never mount a horse or pony without a **hard hat**. It is the most important piece of clothing and should always fit comfortably.

• A **skull cap** (crash helmet) is stronger and tougher than a hard hat. It is designed so that the outer casing, not the rider's head, absorbs the force of a blow. It should feel light and comfortable to wear, as well as being strong.

Footwear

Good boots are important. They should have small heels and smooth soles.

• **Long leather** or **rubber boots** are normally worn with breeches.

• **Top boots** are long black leather hunting boots with brown tops.

• **Jodhpur boots** are short boots (just above ankle height) worn with jodhpurs.

• **Western boots** are mid-calf length and they are often decorated.

*Bandages, 43; Coronet, 10; Cross-country, 78; Dressage, 74; Fetlock joints, 10; Hacking, 66; Hock, 10; Leg aid, 68; Pastern, 10; Showing, 82

Hard hat

Body protector

Jumping whip

String gloves

Breeches

Long boots

Jodhpurs

• A rider will feel more comfortable wearing either **jodhpurs** or **breeches** specially designed for riding. Breeches end at mid-calf, while jodhpurs end just below the ankle. They should fit close to the inside leg, so as not to crease and rub.

*Show jumping, 76; Tendons, 11; Training, 62; Western riding, 72

Body protector

• The **body protector** consists of padding to cushion the rider in the event of falls or kicks. It is worn especially in more dangerous activities such as jumping and *cross-country riding**.

Gloves

• **Gloves** should fit well and allow a sensitive feel on the reins. They may be string, leather, wool with rubber palms, or synthetic.

Jackets

• **Jackets** for competitions should be comfortable and warm and should fit properly so that they do not restrict movement. The jacket should be of good quality and have a vent at the back so that it hangs correctly.

Chaps

• **Chaps** are leather pants without a seat. They are worn over jeans to give extra protection against thorns, rain, heat and cold. They are usually worn for *Western riding**, but they are also popular for casual riding and *hacking**.
• **Half chaps** are a shorter version, from the rider's knees down to the ankles.

Stock

• A **stock** (hunting tie) is a long, white, linen or cotton neckcloth knotted around the neck. It is worn for formal riding, such as *showing*, dressage** or *show jumping**.

Spurs

• **Spurs** should be used by skilled riders only. They can reinforce the *leg aid**, and should be made of metal with blunt ends.

Whips

• **Whips** are used to reinforce the rider's leg aid. They can also be used to correct a horse, but never in anger.
• **Jumping/hacking whip** (standard): about 0.74m (2ft 6in) long. For general use and jumping.
• **Dressage whip**: about 0.91m (3ft) long. Used for *training** and dressage.
• **Hunting whip**: should always be carried with its thong and lash up. It is used in hunting, to help the rider when opening and shutting gates, and to keep hounds off the heels of the horse.

Jumping whip

Dressage whip

Hunting whip

Thong

45

⊞ Fields and fencing

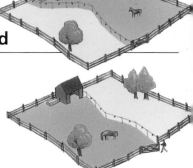

Horses that live outdoors are usually kept in smaller areas than they would roam in the wild. It is important to keep the grass in good condition, so the horses have enough to eat.

Grazing conditions

The quality of a field is affected by its location, the type of grasses grown, its size, the number of horses grazing and time of the year.

• Meadow *forage** is known as **keep**. Old, well-established pastures provide the best grazing because they contain a mixture of grasses and herbs to supply the horse's vitamin and mineral needs.

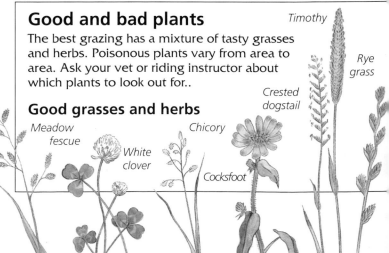

A mixture of grasses and herbs is best.

• The level of acidity of the soil determines the quality of the grasses growing, and their ability to acquire minerals from the soil.

• The ideal amount of grazing is usually one horse per acre. But a lot depends on the size of the horses, the length of time they are out, the quality of the grazing itself, the drainage of the land and the type of soil.

Looking after the field

• The best way of looking after a pasture is to divide the field into two or three parts. Each part has a period of grazing then a period of rest. This is called **rotation**.

• **Good drainage** is important, as waterlogged soil produces poor grass. In winter the field can become very muddy, especially if the soil has a lot of clay in it.

• To keep grass healthy in larger fields, a chain harrow with spikes is pulled across. This is called **harrowing**.

Harrowing

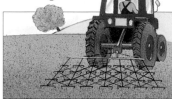

The spikes catch and drag away any dead grass. The goal is to rake the field and prevent the dead grass from building up and stifling the growth of new grass shoots.

• If a small field is fouled by droppings so that there is little to eat, it is described as

horsesick. Droppings should be removed every day, to conserve the pasture and limit the parasites that can cause illness.

• **Fertilizers** encourage healthy grass growth and ensure the correct balance of minerals and nutrients.

• **Rolling** levels the ground which may be muddy and broken up after winter. It also helps push seeds and fertilizers into the soil.

Rolling

• **Topping** the field involves cutting the tops off the plants and grasses. This prevents faster-growing grasses from stifling slower-growing stems and encourages strong roots.

Good and bad plants

The best grazing has a mixture of tasty grasses and herbs. Poisonous plants vary from area to area. Ask your vet or riding instructor about which plants to look out for..

Good grasses and herbs

Timothy

Rye grass

Crested dogstail

Chicory

Meadow fescue

White clover

Cocksfoot

*Forage, 119

For a link to a website where you can see an illustrated guide to plants that are dangerous to horses, go to **www.usborne-quicklinks.com**

Fencing

A field should be surrounded by a strong fence or hedge. The risk of injury to a horse is greater than to other types of animals because the horse might jump the fence. The fence should be at least 1.2m (4ft) high. Always check that there are no nails or other sharp objects sticking out of it, or gaps where the horse could escape. There are different types of fences.

• **Wire** is the most common and one of the cheaper types of fencing. Only smooth, plain and rust-proof wire should be used. Use 5-6 strands. The lowest strand should be not less than 50cm (1ft 8ins) above ground. If it is too low, horses can catch their feet in it. The strands must be kept taut to prevent any injuries.

• A **hedge** is the best way to surround a field, if strong and well-maintained. The thicker and pricklier, the better. Thin hedges should have a fence placed on the inside.

• Wooden **post and rail fences** are the best choice, but they are usually expensive to erect.
• Strong **plastic fencing** is a modern, safe alternative.

• **Stone walls** can be very attractive, but they are very expensive and need to be well maintained. Walls offer good shelter and act as a good wind break.

• An **electric fence** will give a small shock so the horse will not try to push through it. Bright plastic strips should be placed at intervals so that it can be clearly seen.

Extra features

• A **shelter** gives all-year-round protection from the weather. Ideally, it should be built in one corner of the field, with its back to the wind.
• **Water** should always be provided when the horses are kept outside. A long, strong **trough** with no sharp edges is the best way of containing the water. You should make sure that the water is fresh.

• **Gates** should be hung properly so that they swing easily and smoothly and shut firmly. They should also be wide enough so that the horse and rider can walk through comfortably side-by-side.

Poisonous plants and trees

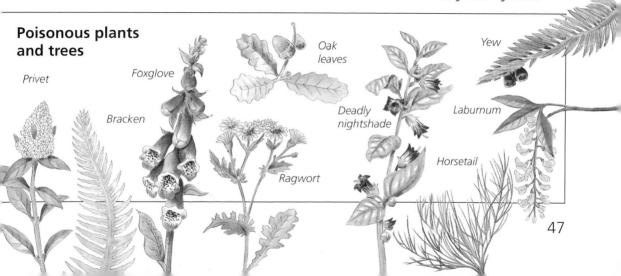

Privet

Foxglove

Bracken

Oak leaves

Ragwort

Deadly nightshade

Laburnum

Horsetail

Yew

47

Barns and stalls

Many horses spend a lot of time in **barns**, especially during winter months. Barns must therefore be warm and comfortable and, above all else, clean, sweet-smelling and well-ventilated. A horse needs to see what is going on, so that he does not become bored.

Indoor accommodation

There are two main types of barn accommodation used today - standing stalls and stalls.

Standing stalls allow the horse to move around.

In stalls, the horses are tied up separately.

More horses can be kept in stalls.

The horse can be left untied.

Standing stalls

A **standing stall** is the best sort of accommodation for horses. It should be large enough for the horse to move around easily, lie down and get up again.
• It should ideally measure at least 4m (12ft) square, with a ceiling no lower than 4m (12ft).

Stalls

Stalls should have strong, solid partitions to prevent fighting between the horses kept in them.
• A building divided into stalls can take more horses than a standing stall, they save labor and *bedding**.
• A disadvantage of stalls is that the horses need to be tied up all the time, to prevent them from escaping. As a result, they can easily become bored, as they cannot look out.
• The horses' access to fresh air is also more limited in stalls than in a loose box.

Inside the barn

• **Stall doors** should be in two halves, with the upper part opening to allow the horse to look out and see what is going on around him, and to let in fresh air.
• The door should be at least 1.5m (4ft 6in) wide and 2m (6ft 6in) high. Narrow doors can be dangerous and cause injuries.

• **Windows** should open at the top to provide fresh air. They should open upward, so preventing drafts blowing into the barn.
• Windows should have bars or netting on the inside so that the glass cannot be broken by the horse.

• **Floors** inside a barn should not be too smooth. This reduces the risk of the horse slipping. Floors should slope slightly away from the door toward a small drain.
• **Anti-cast grooves** on the walls help the horse to get up if he becomes *cast**.
• **Rubber flooring** provides the horse with good leg protection, and it is also hygienic and easy to clean.

*Bedding, 50; Cast, 118

For a link to a website where you can enjoy a virtual tour of some facilities for horses, go to **www.usborne-quicklinks.com**

Fixtures and fittings in the barn

There should be as few fixtures and fittings in the barn as possible, so that they don't take up much room and the horse or his *clothing** won't get caught on them.

• **Latches** on the door should be easy for people to use, but difficult for horses to open. There should be one at the top of the door and one at the bottom.

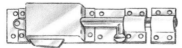

• Wooden **kickboards** should be placed around the inside walls up to 1.5m (4ft 6in) high. They are designed to protect the horse's limbs from injury if he kicks the walls.

• **Tie rings** are metal rings which are attached to barn walls and used for securing horses. They must be firmly fixed. There should be one ring positioned about 1.5m (4ft 6in) high to which the horse can be tied. The ring should be placed on the wall where the horse will be groomed and tacked up.

• A **rope and sinker** is used to secure a horse in a stall, so that he can lie down without getting his legs tangled up. The horse is tied to a rope which passes through a ring. A sinker is attached to the free end of the rope, so that it is never slack and hanging in loops.

• **Cross-tying** is a method of securing a horse by means of attaching two lead ropes or chains, known as **pillar reins**, to posts or pillars. Cross-tying is often used to secure horses in barns or outside. The horse is positioned between the two posts or two walls, roughly 2m (6ft 6in) apart. Cross-tying is also used when transporting a horse in a trailer which has no partition inside.

• A **hay feeder** is used for feeding a horse. It should be placed on the wall in one corner of the barn, about 1m (3ft 3in) from the floor.

• All **electrical fittings** must be placed out of reach of the horse. Electric lighting should be positioned so that it gives the most light and as little shadow as possible.

• All **switches** should be placed outside the stall. They should be designed so that the horse cannot be electrocuted.

• A **fire extinguisher** is an essential piece of equipment, as there are many flammable materials inside a barn. It should be kept well out of the horse's reach, but it must also be in an easily accessible position so that it can be used quickly in an emergency.

Outside the barn

The area outside the barn or stall should also be well-planned. It should be open to fresh air, but sheltered from winds. There should be lots of natural light, with a safe electrical circuit for night lighting. There should be good drainage.

• A **feedroom** should be located near or in the barn. It should contain vermin-proof bins for storing food. Hay and straw should be kept on wooden pallets to allow air to circulate and prevent them from getting damp.

Tackroom

• The **tackroom** should be dry, and big enough to keep all the tack, horse clothing and cupboards for medicines. There should be space for cleaning tack and airing equipment, and some heating for winter.

Stabled horses

A horse should be given fresh and comfortable surroundings. He needs lots of clean bedding (straw, peat moss, wood shavings), which should be changed regularly. It is not good if he stands for long periods on a hard, bare floor.

Types of bedding

A stabled horse needs plenty of **bedding** for day and night. Bedding is used to provide the horse with warmth and to prevent him from injuring himself when he lies down. It should also provide good drainage. It should be dry and soft and not irritate his skin, and discourage him from eating it.

Straw
- **Wheat straw** is the best straw bedding, as it is light and drains well and is less dusty than others.
- **Oat straw** can be tasty, so horses may eat it.
- **Barley straw** tends to be prickly and can irritate a horse's skin. It may also cause the horse *colic** if it is eaten.

Straw

Wood shavings
Wood shavings make a warm, comfortable form of bedding. Clean and inedible, they are good for horses who eat their straw bedding or have allergies to dust.

Wood shavings

Peat moss
Peat moss must be laid thickly, damp patches removed and the bed raked over daily. Warm and comfortable, but it is expensive.

Peat moss

Shredded paper
Shredded paper is warm and dust-free. But some horses are allergic to the ink. The paper also becomes very heavy when damp.

Shredded paper

Deep litter bedding
Deep litter bedding is an alternative to a fresh bed each day (see opposite page). New bedding is put down to cover earlier layers. The stall is cleaned out when the bed becomes too high. Straw, shavings, paper or peat can be used. Droppings must be removed regularly, and fresh bedding added.
- Advantages: less bedding is needed; it provides a warm bed which does not need to be changed each day.
- Disadvantage: the whole bed needs to be dug out and replaced every six months.

Sawdust
Sawdust makes a comfortable and cheap bed. However, it does not make as good a bed as the others, and therefore it is not often used. A disadvantage is that sawdust clogs when soiled and damp and becomes heavy to handle.

Sawdust

For a link to a website where you can find out more about different types of bedding, go to **www.usborne-quicklinks.com**

Mucking out

Barns must be **mucked out** - cleaned out - at least once a day, the beds remade and kept neat and clean. This is an important job which must be done as a daily routine with all stabled horses and ponies.

The daily routine

Each day, in the morning, the droppings and soiled bedding should be removed, the floor swept and the bed shaken up and leveled. This keeps the bedding soft and, with shavings, paper and peat, stops it from becoming packed down and soggy.

Each week the floor should be swept clean, disinfected, and allowed to dry.

Stripping a stall

Laying a new bed is called **stripping a stall**. Any old bedding that is kept should be put down first and the fresh, clean bedding mixed in.

Bedding should be well mixed in when making up the bed. This freshens it up and makes it comfortable.

Bedding down

When the bed is ready for the night, it is known as **bedded down**. To prevent injury and drafts, the bedding should be banked up thickly around the sides.

Bedding should be thicker around the edges than on the floor.

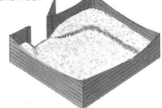

The new bedding should look warm and inviting to the horse or pony.

Mucking out

Every time you visit the stall, any horse droppings should be removed. This task is known as **mucking out**.

This is done by lifting the bedding from underneath and tipping the droppings into a basket or tub called a **muck tub**.

The bedding should be turned and droppings lifted with a pitchfork.

Equipment

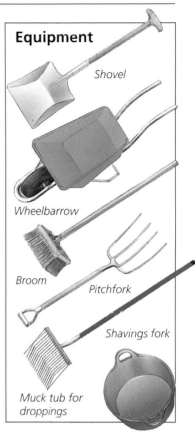

Shovel

Wheelbarrow

Broom

Pitchfork

Shavings fork

Muck tub for droppings

The muckheap

Old bedding and droppings, known as **manure**, are placed on a **muckheap**. You should have three piles.
- **1.** The oldest pile should consist of rotted manure which can be used on the garden.
- **2.** The second pile will be rotting. No more manure should be added to this pile.
- **3.** The third pile is for fresh manure added daily.

The manure piles should be kept neat inside low walls.

*Colic, 58   51

 Feeding

Horses and ponies kept indoors need to eat at least three times a day. The biggest meal should be the last one of the day. Horses like a routine, and they should eat at the same times every day whenever possible. Different types of food suit different types of horses.

Feeding rules

The amount of food horses eat varies according to their type and size. Each horse should be fed according to age, temperament, condition and work load.
• Horses need about 1-1.1 kg (2-2½ lbs) of food per 45 kg (100 lbs) of body weight, while ponies need about 0.6-1 kg (1½-2 lbs) of food per 45kg of body weight.
• Feed in small quantities and often.
• Allow at least an hour after feeding before exercise.
• Ensure a constant supply of fresh water.
• Do not waste expensive food and ensure each horse receives his correct ration.

Compound feeds

Cubes are small pellets of dried food. They provide a balanced diet of the vitamins and minerals which are sometimes missing from grains and hay.
• A **coarse mix** contains cereals and pellets, with a mixture of vitamins and minerals. The cereals have been cooked, which makes them easier for horses to digest.

Oats

Cubes

Barley

Coarse mix

Maize

Concentrates

Oats provide the most balanced diet. They should be fed crushed or bruised rather than whole. The quantity fed to the horse always depends on the amount and type of work to be done by the horse. But oats also make some horses hot, or become excited, so for this reason they should not be fed to children's ponies.
• **Barley** is also a very useful feed, and good for putting weight on thin horses. Horses do not get so hot on barley.
• **Maize** is cooked and flaked. It should not be fed on its own as it is starchy and can make some horses excitable.

Grasses and hay

Grass used to be known by some people as "Dr. Green" as it makes a very good general food.
• The best grass mixture contains types such as rye grass, timothy and crested dogstail, with a small amount of clover.

Grass

There are three main kinds of **hay** (dried grass). Horses should never be fed moldy or musty hay.
• **Seed** or **mixture hay** is cut from specially sown fields. It is usually weed-free, high quality and expensive.

Timothy grass

• **Meadow hay** is cut from permanent pastures. It can vary in quality, but should contain a mixture of grasses and herbs.
• **Clover hay**, like seed hay, is very nutritious, but it can be too rich for ponies.

Meadow grass

Clover

Bulk feeds

- **Bran** has little nutritional value, but it has good fiber content and is sometimes added to feeds in small quantities to bulk them out. It makes adding medicines easier.

Bran

Sugar beet pulp

Chaff

- **Sugar beet** is high in fiber and sugars. It adds bulk when added to other feeds, but it must not be fed without water.
- **Chaff** is chopped hay or straw. Although it is rarely used in the U.S., it can be added to poor-quality hay to give it extra bulk. Chaff also encourages chewing.

Cooked foods

- **Linseed jelly**, made by boiling linseed seeds, is good for fattening up horses and putting a shine on their coats. But linseed can be poisonous, unless it is correctly cooked first. It must be fed within 24 hours of preparation, or else it should be thrown away.
- The thinner **linseed tea** is made in the same way as the jelly, but with more water. It can be given as a warm drink to a tired or sick horse.

- **Oatmeal gruel** (a type of thick drink) is fed cool to horses. It is a useful drink for tired horses when they return to their stalls after heavy exercise.
- **Boiled barley** is easily digested. The grain should be boiled for 2-3 hours until it is soft. It can then be fed warm and mixed with another feed.

- **Haylage** is a cross between hay and *silage**. It is dust-free and good for horses with breathing problems. But in order to avoid causing any digestive upsets, haylage should be gradually added to the horse's diet over a period of 2-3 weeks.

- **Alfalfa**, also called **lucerne**, is an alternative to the usual hay. It is a tall green plant with a purple flower. The food is prepared in the same way as hay but is more nutritious. It is also very expensive.

Alfalfa

Feeding equipment

Scales weigh the food.

Feed scoop is used for measuring out food.

Automatic waterer provides fresh water.

Buckets are most commonly used for water.

A **hay net** is used when traveling.

A **hay feeder** is used in barns.

Food supplements

- **Vitamins** and **minerals** are needed for growth and good health. Good pasture and sunshine supply some of them and the body makes others. A **solid lick**, or block, hung up in the barn provides vitamins and minerals lacking in the horse's diet.
- **Molasses** is a thick brown sugar syrup, and is very nutritious. As it is so tasty, it can be very useful in persuading bad *keepers**. It should be diluted with a little warm water and then mixed with the feed.

Solid lick

Grooming and clipping

Stabled horses should ideally be **groomed** every day, for about one hour. This keeps their skin healthy, tones their muscles and puts a shine on their coats.

How horses groom themselves

Horses kept outside groom themselves. Grooming is a form of social behavior and is used to relieve itches. The oils and greases in horses' coats keep them waterproof and warm. They can roll if they feel itchy or they are sweaty. They can rub their bodies against trees to help them shed their coats in spring and autumn.

Grooming equipment

Each item used in grooming has a different purpose.

A **dandy brush** has tough, long bristles to remove mud on an unclipped horse. Never use on thin-skinned or tickly parts.

A **body brush** is the main brush, used to remove dust and grease. Shorter, softer bristles reach through the coat to the skin below.

A **curry comb** of rubber or metal is used for clearing dust and grease from the body brush, by scraping it against the brush.

A **water brush** is long and narrow, with short bristles. Used damp with water, for laying the mane and tail after brushing.

Separate **sponges** are used with warm water to clean around the eyes, nostrils and dock.

A **hoof pick** is used to remove any dirt and stones from the hooves. This should be done at least twice a day, and before and after exercise.

Hoof oil protects the hoof wall and gives it a nice finish. A thin coat should be painted on the wall right up to the coronet*, and on the sole.

A **sweat scraper** is used to remove excess sweat or water from the horse's coat.

Strapping pads made of stuffed leather are used for strapping. Wisps made of hay were traditionally used for this work.

A **mane and tail comb** made of aluminum or plastic is used only for thinning the tail and when braiding the mane and tail.

The daily grooming

Most horses enjoy being groomed and learn to cooperate. But they should always be treated with consideration and patience.

Picking out feet

Start the daily grooming session by picking out the feet. A *muck tub** should be used to catch all the dirt.

- **1.** Pick up each foot in turn. Remove all the dirt with the hoof pick. Work down from the heel to the toe, with the pick pointing away from you. This avoids penetrating any soft areas on the hoof.
- **2.** Clean the cleft of the *frog** and look for any signs of *thrush**. Check the *shoe** to see if it is tight and that no *clenches** are rising.

Strapping

Strapping is a complete grooming after exercise while the skin pores are open.

- **1.** Starting with the neck, groom all the near (left) side thoroughly. Use the body brush and rubber curry comb. Repeat on the off (right) side.

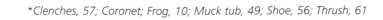

For a link to a website where you can play a fun game that shows you how to groom a pony, go to **www.usborne-quicklinks.com**

• **2.** With the strapping pad, bang the muscles, bringing it down firmly on *quarters**, shoulders and neck. Do this for about 10 minutes on each side: this tones up muscles and puts a shine on the coat.

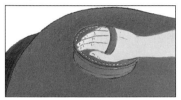

• **3.** Gently groom the face with a body brush or cloth.

• **4.** Use a damp water brush on the mane and tail. Finally, polish the coat with a cotton cloth called a **rub rag**. This helps to remove any surface dust.

When finished, the coat should look shiny.

Stand to the side to avoid kicks.

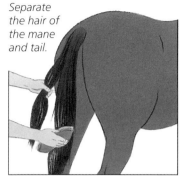

Separate the hair of the mane and tail.

• **5.** Brush the mane and tail with the body brush.
• **6.** Paint some hoof oil on the hooves.

Quartering

Quartering is a quick grooming before exercise. Use the body brush on a clipped horse. (Dandy brushes are too prickly.)
• **1.** Pick out the feet.
• **2.** Sponge the eyes, nostrils and dock.
• **3.** Fold the front of his blanket back. Groom from the head, replace blanket and groom hindquarters.
• **4.** Finally, brush out the mane and tail.

The horse should be secured with a halter and lead rope.

Clipping

Horses change, or **shed**, their coats twice a year, in spring and autumn. In winter they grow thick coats to keep them warm. Clipping every 2-6 weeks prevents a horse from getting hot and helps it to work better.
• With a **full clip**, the whole of the horse's coat is clipped, including the legs.
• The **hunter clip** leaves the hair on the legs, from the thigh downward. This protects the legs against scratches. A saddle-patch is left on the back to prevent the horse's skin being rubbed by the saddle.
• The **trace clip** is one in which the horse is clipped under the neck, on the flanks and on the belly. For horses which are kept outside.
• With a **bib clip**, only the horse's chest and throat are clipped. Good for a horse which lives outside a lot.
• A **blanket clip** involves clipping the horse all over, except on his loins, back and legs. This type of clip helps a hard-working horse to keep cool.

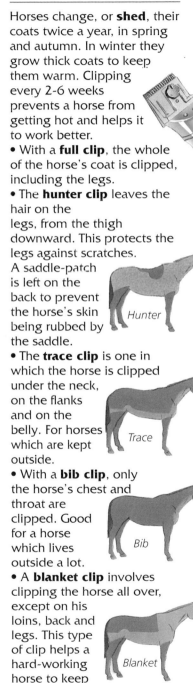

Hunter

Trace

Bib

Blanket

*Quarters, 10   55

Shoeing

A horse walking on hard roads needs his feet protected by metal **shoes**. Shoes protect the walls of the hoof, and stop it from wearing away. But the hooves are always growing and need to be trimmed, or the horse can become lame. A horse should normally have his shoes replaced every 4-6 weeks by a **blacksmith** or **farrier**.

Anvil

Shoeing equipment

In order to fit the shoe, the farrier needs a number of different tools. Below are the main ones used.

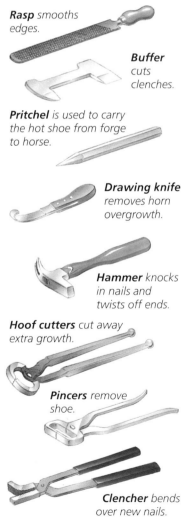

Rasp smooths edges.

Buffer cuts clenches.

Pritchel is used to carry the hot shoe from forge to horse.

Drawing knife removes horn overgrowth.

Hammer knocks in nails and twists off ends.

Hoof cutters cut away extra growth.

Pincers remove shoe.

Clencher bends over new nails.

Types of shoes

There are different types of shoes to suit the many different horses and the sort of work they do.

• The **plain stamped shoe** is the simplest type. It consists of a plain bar of iron, which is shaped, stamped with nail holes, and given a toe-clip. Designed for slow work.

• The **hunter shoe** is used by a horse moving quickly on grass and pulling up short. It is made of *concave** iron, to prevent suction and to give better grip on soft ground.

• The **feather-edged shoe** is used for horses that brush (hit) the opposite leg. The inside branch is "feathered" - has a straighter edge - and fits close under the *hoof wall**. This reduces the risk of the metal edge hitting the opposite leg.

• The **grass tip** is a thin, half-length shoe. It protects the toe area of the wall from splitting. It keeps the *frog** healthy when the horse is not working.

• In the **rolled toe shoe**, the toe is bevelled (sloped). It is used if a horse drags his feet or stumbles.

• The **surgical shoe** is a special type used for problems such as *corns**, *laminitis** and injured *tendons**. There are many different versions.

• The **racing plate** is a very lightweight shoe made of aluminum. It is designed for *racing** horses or *show** ponies, and should be used only on soft surfaces, such as grass or sand.

• **Calkins** are raised projections on the heels of a shoe. They are designed to help increase the shoe's grip on the ground.

Parts of a shoe

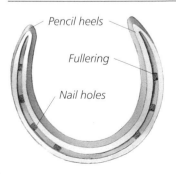

Pencil heels

Fullering

Nail holes

Concave, 118; Corns, 61; Frog, 10; Laminitis, 61; Racing, 84; Showing, 82; Tendons, 11; Hoof wall, 10

For a link to a website containing helpful tips from a farrier about shoeing your horse, go to **www.usborne-quicklinks.com**

Types of studs

Metal studs can be attached to a shoe heel to reduce the risk of slipping.
• **Road studs** have hard metal centers which give a firm grip on the ground.

They are attached when the horse is **shod** (has his shoes attached), and they are meant to remain in the shoe.
• **Competition studs** are used only on grass, not on roads. They should be removed after use.

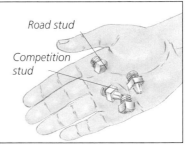

Road stud

Competition stud

Stages in shoeing

The ideal method of shoeing is called **hot shoeing**. In this, the shoe is specially made to fit the foot. It is tried on while it is still hot, so adjustments can be made before it is nailed on.
• **Cold shoeing** involves fitting a shoe which has already been made. Only minor adjustments can then be made to its shape.

hoof cutters. A rasp is then used to give the foot a smooth and level surface.

Hoof cutters remove extra growth.

has no feeling so this does not hurt. Any adjustments to the shoe can now be made.

Nailing

The shoe is cooled in water and nailed on. The nail points stick out of the hoof, and are twisted off, leaving small pieces called **clenches**, which are nailed downward.

Nailing on the new shoe

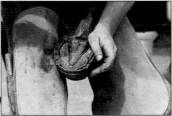

Removal

The old shoe is removed by cutting the clenches (see Nailing) with a buffer and hammer, and levering off the shoe with pincers. Clenches should be well cut, to avoid damage to the hoof wall.

Pincers lever off the old shoe.

Preparation

The *sole** and frog are cleaned out by the farrier. The extra growth of the hoof wall is clipped off with the

Fitting

The hot shoe is pressed on to the hoof, to make sure it fits exactly. The wall of the hoof

The new shoe is pressed on the hoof to check for size.

Finishing

Finally, the farrier rasps the outside of the hoof and the clenches. This ensures that there are no sharp edges.

All edges smoothed by rasp

Clench

*Sole, 10   57

Illness and injury

A healthy horse is a happy horse. He will be bright and lively, stand well and have a shiny coat, alert eyes and ears. Dull eyes, tiredness and a generally unhappy appearance all indicate poor health.

Digestive illnesses

• **Colic** is a pain in the horse's *abdomen**. It is often caused by indigestion from changes in diet, working too soon after eating, or by worms. Colic can be fatal, and a vet should be called immediately if you suspect that a horse may be suffering from it. The diet should be changed or the horse treated for worms.

• **Worms** are one of the most common causes of poor health. Red, white, pin, lung and tapeworms can be the worst. They can cause tail-rubbing, coughing, colic, *anemia**, blood clots, and even death. Worms should be controlled by dosing with a worming medicine every six to eight weeks.

• **Lampas** is a swollen condition of the gums or roof of the mouth. The membrane on the roof of the mouth secretes a lubricating fluid called mucus. This discomfort may make it painful for the horse to eat properly. This can make him lose condition.

Lampas may be caused by a dietary imbalance. It sometimes occurs when the *incisors** change in young horses.

Sharp teeth may also cause eating difficulties, and they should be regularly checked by a vet or equine dentist.

Outward signs can indicate a horse's health, and it is important to recognize them.

Worms inside the stomach. They are treated with drugs.

This coat is healthy. A dull coat can indicate poor health.

Small intestine *Stomach*
Large colon
Cutaway diagram showing the inside of a horse's stomach.

A sign of choking is saliva coming from the nose and mouth.

• **Choking** is a serious problem, usually caused by dry food or a hard object becoming stuck in the horse's throat. A vet will be needed to clear the obstruction.

Breathing problems

• **Coughs** can be caused by viral or bacterial infection. These can last for a long time and can be very difficult to get rid of. Some coughs are caused by an allergy to the fungal or other *spores** found in hay and straw. The horse should not work.

A horse with a cough should be given plenty of rest.

• **Broken wind**, also known as **Chronic Obstructive Pulmonary Disease** (**C.O.P.D.**), is caused by an allergic reaction to fungal spores. Rest and antibiotics help, as well as a dust-free environment.
• **Strangles** is a highly contagious disease, mainly found in young horses. A high temperature is followed by nasal discharge, swollen glands and abscesses. The horse should be isolated and treated with antibiotics until completely cured.

• **Equine influenza** is a viral infection. The horse should be isolated and rested. Ideally, all horses should be vaccinated to prevent influenza.

Skin problems

• **Lice** are common on horses in the spring. They make a horse very itchy. His coat will be dull and he may lose weight. Lice powder should be applied over all the affected areas and repeated after two weeks.

Louse

• **Mange** is very contagious and is caused by parasitic mites. Symptoms include itching, oozing scabs and loss of hair. The vet will prescribe special creams or washes to clear the problem.
• **Sweetitch** is a reaction to the bite of a type of midge, active from the month of April through to October. It can be avoided by stabling the horse in the early evening, and by using insect sprays and repellents.

A rubbed tail is often a sign of sweetitch.

• **Warbles** are caused when warble flies lay eggs on the horse's coat. The larvae penetrate the skin, causing painful lumps. The maggots may have to be removed by surgery. The wound must be cleaned and dusted with antiseptic or antibiotic powder.
• **Nettlerash**, or **urticaria**, is usually a sudden allergic reaction to plants, insect bites or changes in food. Severe cases will require veterinary attention.
• **Saddle sores** and **galls** are swellings or wounds on the horse's back. They are caused by the saddle or girth. Any open wounds should be carefully washed, dried and then dusted with antiseptic powder. The horse should not be ridden until the wounds have healed.

• **Ringworm** is a highly contagious fungal infection which can affect humans. The ringworm should be treated with an antifungal dressing and a special medicine added to the feed. The horse should be isolated and all equipment disinfected.

Ringworm causes circular patches on the skin.

• **Cracked heels** and **mud fever** are bacterial infections occurring in wet or muddy conditions. The legs and stomach become covered in scabs which seal in the infection. Clip away hair from the affected areas, clean thoroughly and treat with antibiotic creams.
• **Rainrot** is similar to mud fever, but the skin on the back becomes covered in sores. Treat as for mud fever.

Various illnesses

- **Tetanus**, or **lockjaw**, is a very serious disease, usually fatal. A stiffness sets in, and in the later stages the jaws become locked. Another symptom is the horse's third eyelid half covering the eye. Horses should always be vaccinated against tetanus.

The third eyelid half drawn over the eye.

- **Eye infections** can be serious so a vet should always be consulted. Antibiotics help to stop infection and limit any damage. Each eye should be cleaned with a separate swab of cotton soaked in a saline solution.

*A **fly fringe** helps to keep flies away.*

- With **azoturia**, the horse's muscles become stiff and painful and the muscle fibers and kidneys can be damaged. This can happen during exercise, especially after a day off. The horse must not be moved. A vet will give a sedative and anti-inflammatory drugs.

Leg problems

- **Splints** are small, bony lumps which appear on the upper part of the splint bone and cannon bone. They are more common in young horses, 3-4 years old. They are caused by strain or a blow, mineral imbalance or a fracture. To treat, the horse should be rested, cold hosed three times a day and then have a kaolin poultice (see opposite) applied. Anti-inflammatory drugs may also be prescribed by the vet.
- **Windgalls** are swellings which appear on either side of and just above the fetlock joint. They are a blemish, but rarely cause trouble. To treat, the horse should be rested and cold hosed.
- **Bog spavins** are soft, non-painful swellings on the upper inside of the hock. They are not serious, but they show that there is strain on the legs. The horse should be treated as for windgalls, with rest and cold hosing.

- **Capped elbows** and **hocks** are swellings under the skin which are caused by rubbing or kicking. Cold hosing may help to reduce the swelling.
- **Broken knees** are often caused by stumbling or falling. A vet should be called to check the legs.
- **Strained tendons** can be caused when the fibers in the tendons which connect muscles to bones become strained. This causes pain and lameness. The horse should be treated by a vet. The treatment may include cold hosing, poulticing and anti-inflammatory drugs.

Tendons of the foreleg

- **Brushing** is the name given to wounds on the the fetlock joint caused by one shoe hitting the opposite foot. *Brushing boots** and good *shoeing** will help prevent this occurring.

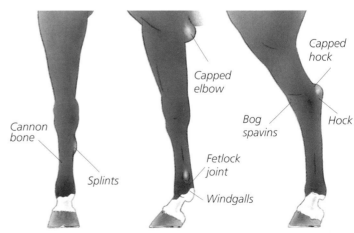

Foreleg - front *Foreleg - side* *Hind leg - side*

Cannon bone

Splints

Capped elbow

Fetlock joint

Windgalls

Capped hock

Bog spavins

Hock

Brushing boot, 44; Shoeing, 56

Foot problems

• **Lameness** can be caused by a number of things, such as *poor conformation**, bad riding, corns or stones stuck in the feet. If a horse is lame, a vet should always be consulted.

• **Navicular** is a serious form of arthritis which can lead to lameness. The navicular bone at the back of the foot becomes rough, which inflames the flexor tendon beneath it. It can be caused by concussion or by poor conformation.

• **Laminitis** is a very painful inflammation of the laminae connecting the inner, sensitive structures of the foot to the outer, insensitive structures. It is caused by a rich diet, obesity, or too much exercise on hard roads. Shoes should be taken off and the feet cold hosed.

Laminitis makes it very painful to stand.

The vet can then give anti-inflammatory injections and pain killers.

• **Thrush** is a disease in the frog of the foot which creates a foul smell. It is usually caused by dirty and damp conditions and not picking the feet out regularly. The feet should be picked out, cleaned and, if necessary, treated with a poultice.

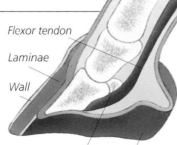

Flexor tendon

Laminae

Wall

Navicular bone   *Frog*
Cross section of a horse's hoof

• **Seedy toe** is a separation of the wall of the hoof from the sole at the toe, leaving a hollow. It is caused by damage to the foot followed by an infection. A vet should pare back the horn and dress the wound.

• **Sandcrack** appears in the wall of the hoof, growing from the *coronet** downward. It is caused by damage to the coronary band. A vet and blacksmith should treat it. A clip can be placed across the crack, to prevent it from spreading and to allow it to grow out.

Sandcrack on a hoof

Diagram showing where problems occur on the base of the hoof.

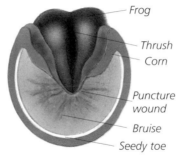

Frog

Thrush

Corn

Puncture wound

Bruise

Seedy toe

• **Hot nail** is caused by the farrier driving a nail too close to the sensitive laminae of the foot. The nail should be removed immediately.

With a **pricked sole**, a nail has actually pierced the sensitive structures. The shoe should be removed, and then the foot poulticed.

Treatments

• **Poultices** are made from different substances, such as kaolin or bran. They are applied moist on the skin for different purposes.

Applied hot under bandages, they relieve sprains and strains, and soothe bruising and swelling. Put on cuts and wounds, they help to draw out any dirt and infected matter.

A poultice sock

• **Cold hosing**, which involves gently trickling cold water over the injured part, is good for treating bruises, swelling and sprains, and for clearing wounds.

• **Hot compresses** are used for treating pain or swelling and where a poultice cannot be used. It consists of a towel soaked in hot salt water and gently pressed on the injured part.

*Poor conformation, 18; Coronet, 10   61

Training

The first stages in training a horse or pony to accept a rider on his back are known as **breaking**. He can then be trained to respond to the rider's *aids**. All stages in training should be taught slowly, calmly, and firmly, but without force.

Teaching foals

A foal should become used to human contact. Beginning at his neck, then his back and quarters, gently touch him all over. It may take several days before he accepts this touching.

Leading

You can teach a foal to be led without pulling away on a rein or rope. This is called **leading**. At first he should be led with the mare.

• He must first learn to accept a small halter of soft leather known as a **foalslip**.

• Alternatively, a special **foal halter** can be used to hold and lead the foal. It must be soft and fit well, and must be knotted so that it does not pull right up onto his head.

Halter

Tying up

Gradually, the foal can be taught to be tied up. This is best done with a rope with a *quick-release knot**.

Hoof trimming

A foal needs to have his feet trimmed regularly. Early on he should be taught to pick up each foot in turn.

Weaning

When a foal is about 6 months old, he is taken away from his mother's milk and fed on new food. This is known as **weaning**. He may get very upset at this stage, but will soon get over missing his mother.

Breaking

If a horse has been handled gently as a foal, he should accept a rider. This part of his education is known as **breaking**, and takes place when he is 3-4 years old.

• He should accept a *roller**, then a saddle.

• Next, the bit should be placed in the horse's mouth. This is an important stage, as the bit is one of the means by which a rider communicates with the horse.

Longeing

The horse circles around the trainer.

To teach a horse to balance himself and improve his *gaits**, rhythm and *impulsion**, he is sent around on the end of a longe rein. This is called **longeing**. It teaches him to understand verbal commands, and strengthens his muscles without a rider's weight on his back.

Longeing equipment

Padded roller is used before a saddle.

Longe whip should be as long but as light as possible.

Galloping boots are used to protect the legs from knocks.

Breast-plate

Longe cavesson, a padded adjustable noseband

Longe rein at least 7m (23ft) and made of strong webbing

Snaffle bit

Side reins are used to introduce the horse to the feel of rein contact.

*Aids, 68; Gaits, 70; Impulsion, 120; Quick-release knot, 43; Roller, 42

For a link to a website where you can find some advice on how to train your horse to jump, go to **www.usborne-quicklinks.com**

Long reining

Long reining can be used after longeing to teach a horse more about the aids. Two long reins are used to drive him ahead, or turn him.

Backing

Backing is the stage when the horse actually accepts a rider on his back.

• Run your hands over his back until he is relaxed.

• Slowly lean against him with your weight across his back.

• Place a foot in the stirrup and slowly put some weight on it. This helps him to get used to weight.

• If he is relaxed, you can now mount fully.

Riding the horse

In order to teach the horse or pony to **take the bit**, he should be ridden forward at a walk. The impulsion should then be increased with stronger leg aids.

• As he moves forward, the rider should give voice commands so the horse associates them with the action of leg aids.

Using the rein and leg aid to turn

Turning away

To teach the horse to make a simple smooth turn, the rider should move the inside rein wide to indicate direction. The aids used are: **inside leg** - for impulsion; **outside leg** - to stop hindquarters moving outward; **inside hand** - gives direction and bend; **outside hand** - to control impulsion.

Jumping

Most horses can be easily trained to jump low fences. They can be trained to jump with or without a rider, but they must be taught to jump calmly and confidently.

Ground poles

Begin training by trotting the horse over poles on the ground. Once he is going calmly, he can then be introduced to a simple, low obstacle such as a cross pole.

Longeing over jumps

If a horse is being taught to jump on a longe, he should be positioned so that he approaches the jump straight on.

Free jumping

Free jumping means jumping in an enclosed area without a rider. The horse is controlled from the ground by a trainer and assistants.

First fences

The rider should approach the fence at a *trot** so that the horse has time to organize his movements.

• It helps the horse if a pole is placed on the ground in front of the fence. This helps him to take off in the right place.

The horse approaches the center of the jump.

Bad behavior

A horse which has been well-trained will usually behave well. Some horses behave badly, but problems can be corrected through careful handling and riding. If you do have a problem, you must seek expert help and not try to tackle it on your own.

A bucking horse

Causes

Fear is a major cause of bad behavior in horses and ponies. It often comes from trying to defend themselves.
• Rough handling can lead to biting, kicking or barging. But some horses have aggressive natures and need to be handled firmly.
• Boredom and frustration cause bad behavior. The horse must understand what he is being asked to do. Pain is another major cause.

Toys such as this plastic apple help prevent boredom.

Barn sour

A **barn sour** horse is one which refuses to cooperate with the rider. He may stop dead or turn and run home.
• Keep him moving forward, and use a whip if necessary to reinforce *leg aids**.

If the horse stops, push him on.

Rearing

Rearing is when a horse rises up on his hind legs. If a horse rears, first ask your vet to check that he is not in pain.
• It often happens because the rider asks him to go forward but holds him back with the reins.
• If a horse rears, you must sit forward and not pull on the reins.

If the horse rears, the rider must sit well forward.

As the horse lands, he must be sent forward.

Bucking

Bucking is when the horse jumps vertically, with legs stiff and back arched. The rider can be thrown off the horse's back.
• A horse may buck because the bit or the saddle he is wearing is hurting.
• It is much harder for the horse to buck if he is going forward. If you feel he is about to buck, push him on and keep his head up.

Bolting

Bolting is when a horse suddenly runs off. He usually bolts out of fear.
• The rider should try and persuade the horse to stop, or at least slow down. Put one hand on his neck to help support yourself, and pull and give on the other rein in time with the horse's stride.
• Do not shout at him, but use your voice to give calming commands. Try to turn him in a large circle.

Biting

A **biting** horse will flatten his ears and try to bite anyone who attempts to handle him. This is a very nasty habit which must be stopped as soon as possible.
• Never let a horse or pony get away with biting. Tell him off at once by saying "No" very firmly.
• If you have to, give him a hard slap on the chest or shoulder. Never slap his head, as this will make him nervous and *headshy**.

*Headshy, 119; Leg aids, 68

For a link to a website where you can hear sounds of horses, go to **www.usborne-quicklinks.com**

Kicking

Kicking can become a serious habit that must be stopped before someone gets hurt.

• Some horses may kick because they are ticklish and sensitive when they are being groomed. You must be gentle with them.

• Whenever you handle a horse, make sure that you are close to his side, in the least vulnerable position.

Avoid the hindquarters of a kicking horse.

Cribbing and wind-sucking

Cribbing is when the horse grips something such as the edge of the barn door with his teeth and swallows air.

• Cribbing can develop into **wind-sucking**. This is when the horse sucks in air with a loud "burping" noise, without gripping with his teeth .

• Remove any unnecessary fittings, and paint the edge of the door with an anti-chew liquid, or cover it over with a metal chew strip. Fit the horse with an **anti-cribbing strap**.

Cribbing damages the teeth.

An anti-weave grill fitted to the stall door prevents weaving.

Weaving

With **weaving**, the horse may swing his head from side to side. Or he may rock his whole body, moving from one leg to the other. It is a common problem caused by boredom. An **anti-weave grill** helps prevent it.

• A weaving horse should be turned out of the barn as much as possible and given more exercise.

Chewing

Chewing and tearing clothing and other things inside the barn can be very expensive and can damage a horse's teeth.

• If a horse is a blanket-tearer or chewer, remember to move everything that he could chew out of his reach. If he persists, you can paint the blankets with a special, foul-tasting liquid.

• If this does not work, you could fit a **clothing bib muzzle** to the horse. This attaches to his halter.

Stall walking

Stall walking is when a horse paces around and around his stall. This is also caused by boredom. Stall walking puts strain on his legs and may make him lose weight.

• Turn him out, day and night if possible, covered with a blanket and with a shelter.

• If he has to be kept in some of the time, ensure he has hay to keep him occupied, and that he is not frightened of any neighboring horses.

Rolling

Rolling is a natural, healthy exercise which all horses enjoy. But a horse that rolls may possibly be suffering from *colic**, which means the vet should be called at once.

• If a horse rolls in a stall he may become **cast**. This is when his legs are trapped against the walls and he cannot get up into a standing position. A rope should be put around his legs and he should be rolled back gently. An **anti-cast roller** can prevent this from happening.

A horse that keeps rolling may be sick, and he should be seen by a vet.

English-style riding

English-style riding developed from the old European classical style of riding and is now practiced all over the world. It is a very elegant way of riding a horse. Obedience and a harmonious partnership is the main goal.

Riding arenas

• An **indoor riding arena** is the best place for *training** and *schooling** horses. It is usually rectangular, measuring 40x20m (131x66ft) or more. This is the ideal size for schooling, allowing the horse's balance and agility to be developed.
• An outdoor enclosure or riding arena is called an **outdoor arena**. It is usually rectangular.
• The surfaces of indoor or outdoor arenas can be made of sand, wood chippings or plastic granules.

Hacking

Hacking is the name given to riding for pleasure along roads, as opposed to schooling. With hacking, you need to observe a number of rules. The most important is to be careful when crossing other people's land and property.

Riding in the country

You are allowed to ride on roads, bridle paths and some other special areas.
• Check if you need permission from a landowner.
• Always shut the gates behind you.
• Keep to field edges.
• Never jump any gates, hedges or ditches.

Make sure gates are properly closed.

Riding on the road

Do not ride on the road unless the horse is quiet in traffic.
• Ride on grass shoulders wherever possible.
• Never ride on icy roads.
• Obey the highway laws.
• Children should be accompanied by an adult.
• Wear reflective bands or jackets.
• Always thank considerate drivers by raising your hand.
• Always ride with the flow of traffic and keep to the side. Groups should ride in single file.

Before mounting

Before mounting, check and tighten the girth, in order to prevent the saddle from slipping. (This job should quickly become a habit.)

• Face the saddle and adjust the leathers so the *stirrup iron** reaches to your armpit. Stand in front of the horse to check that the stirrups are level.
• It is important at this stage to check that everything is properly adjusted.

Schooling, 121; Stirrup iron, 37; Training, 62

For a link to a website where you can find a fun page full of animated cartoon horses, go to **www.usborne-quicklinks.com**

Mounting

From the ground

Stand with your left shoulder to the horse's left shoulder. Hold the reins in the left hand and place your left hand in front of the horse's *withers**.
• Hold the stirrup with the right hand and place the ball of your left foot into the stirrup iron.
• Face the horse. Take the waist of the saddle in your right hand, straighten both knees and spring up.
• As you straighten your left leg, swing your right leg up and over the horse's back.

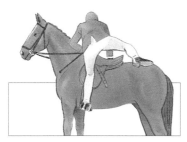

• Sit down gently into the saddle. Once you are in place, put your right foot in the stirrup iron and then hold the reins in both hands.

With assistance

There are two methods of mounting with help.
• With the **leg up** method, a helper places his left hand under the rider's left knee and right hand around the rider's ankle.

The rider springs up off his right foot, while the helper raises the rider's left leg straight up from the knee.
• You can also mount from a **mounting block**. Standing on the block, you mount in the usual way.

Dismounting

The best and the safest way to dismount is to take both feet out of the stirrups so your legs are hanging free.
• Lean slightly forward. Holding the reins in your left hand, put this hand on the horse's mane.
• Place your right hand on the *pommel** of the saddle. Swing your right leg behind you, over the horse's back, and spring off.

After mounting

In order to adjust the stirrup leathers, pull up the loose end of the leather, holding one finger on the tongue of the buckle. You can now move the leather up or down without losing the end.

• Move the buckle under the skirt to prevent rubbing.
• You should always keep your foot in the stirrup and maintain a "good seat" (good position) in the saddle.
• The girth may need tightening again once you are mounted.
• To tighten the girth, move your leg forward, with the foot still in the stirrup, and lift up the saddle flap.
• Pull up the straps, one by one, pushing the tongue of the buckle into a higher hole.

Sit in the lowest part of the saddle, hips square with the horse's hips.

*Pommel, 34; Withers, 10

English-style riding

Holding the reins

Your hands are an important link between you and the horse. The reins should be held just firmly enough to form a contact with the horse's mouth.

A straight line should pass from rider's elbow, through hand, along the reins to the horse's mouth.

• Single reins pass from the bit between your third and fourth fingers, and out between your thumbs and first fingers. Keep your thumbs on top of the reins.

• Two pairs of reins should be held as for the single rein, except that the little finger of each hand should divide the reins. You should keep your hands level with each other, and one on each side of the horse's neck. Your knuckles should face outward, with your thumbs on top.

• Holding the reins in one hand, pass the reins from one hand to the other, so that the second finger divides the reins which you are passing. Buckle ends pass over the index finger, and are held by the thumb.

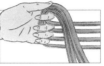

The aids

Aids are the hand or leg signals which the rider uses to tell the horse what to do. *Whips**, *martingales** and s*purs** are artificial aids.

• **Hand aids** help control and guide the horse. The fingers of the inside hand indicate the direction. The fingers of the outside hand control and regulate the speed and *gait**.

• **Leg aids** create *impulsion** in the horse. They also guide and control the horse's hindquarters.

• The rider's back can be used as a **seat aid**, to increase the horse's impulsion.

Exercises

Riding can be very tiring on your body, especially if you are new to it. This is because you are using muscles which are not normally used. Some simple exercises can be done to increase suppleness, and improve posture and balance.

• **Ankle circling** increases suppleness in the ankles. Sit in the saddle, and move your feet around in circles, in one direction then the other.

• **Toe touching** strengthens stomach muscles. With feet in stirrups, bend slowly down and touch your toes. Do on one side and then the other.

• **Swinging arms** increases suppleness in the waist. Facing forward, hold out your arms at shoulder height. Then slowly swing your body around, first to one side and then the other. Do this a few times in long, smooth movements, making sure you keep your balance.

*Gaits, 70; Impulsion, 120; Martingales, 41; Spurs, 45; Whips, 45

Sidesaddle riding

For a link to a website where you can test your knowledge of horses by trying some quizzes, go to www.usborne-quicklinks.com

Sidesaddle riding is a very elegant form of riding. It was devised for women, because people used to think that they should not ride astride. It became less popular after the 19th century, but many people have now become interested again.

The saddle

A specially made saddle is used. It is designed with a flat seat and two pommels.

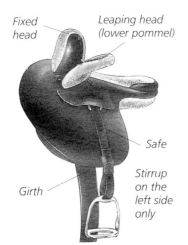

Fixed head

Leaping head (lower pommel)

Safe

Stirrup on the left side only

Girth

Position (the seat)

The rider sits straight up and faces square to the front. Your left foot should be in the stirrup, while your right leg rests over the fixed head of the saddle.
• Hold your right shoulder back in order to sit square.

• For a good position, sit with your weight spread evenly across both seat bones. The outer thigh of the right leg should be in close contact with the saddle. The inside of your right thigh should be pressed firmly into the fixed head, or upper pommel.
• Your left leg should be in a similar position to the one you use for riding astride. It should hang in a relaxed way, but be placed firmly against the horse.
• The reins should be held low down or in the lap, with a straight line from your elbow to the horse's bit.

Adults wear bowler hats.

A heavy skirt called an **apron** is worn over breeches and boots.

Reins held low

A long whip is used to replace the right leg.

Only one blunt spur should be worn.

Mounting

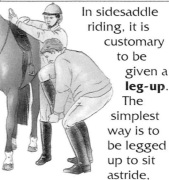

In sidesaddle riding, it is customary to be given a **leg-up**. The simplest way is to be legged up to sit astride, and then swing your right leg over the fixed head. Experienced riders go straight into the sidesaddle position.
• When mounting from a block, place your left foot in the stirrup and take the reins in your left hand. Hold the waist of the saddle and spring upward, turning your left knee so that it is facing the front. You land astride, and bring your right leg over the saddle.

The inside of the right thigh is tucked into the fixed head.

Gaits

The patterns of footsteps a horse makes at various speeds are called **gaits**. In English-style riding, there are four basic gaits: the walk (four-time beat); the trot (two-time); the canter (three-time); the gallop (four-time).

Walk

The **walk** is the most comfortable gait, being calm and steady. The walk has four beats to a stride, so it is called four-time. The legs move in a set sequence, one at a time: left hindleg followed by left fore, right hind, right fore.

Trot

The **trot** is a two-time gait. Bouncy, but it should look and feel calm and rhythmic.

• The horse's legs move in pairs. The near foreleg and off hind leg together, then off foreleg and near hind leg. These are known as **diagonals**.

Canter

The **canter** is a three-time gait. Three hoofbeats are heard at every stride.

• The horse is said to **lead** with a certain leg. Either will do. When going around a corner, though, the inside foreleg should lead, for good balance.

Gallop

The **gallop** is the fastest pace at which a horse moves.

• It is a four-time pace: left hind, right hind, left fore, right fore. On a bend, the inside leg leads.

For a link to a website where you can watch simple animations of different gaits and find out more about them, go to www.usborne-quicklinks.com

Square halt

In a **square halt**, or **standing square**, the horse should stand straight and still. His weight should be spread evenly over his four legs.

• Both fore and hind legs should be placed opposite each other. He should appear alert and ready to move again when he is asked.

Horse and rider at the halt

Jumping

Jumping has five phases.
• At the **approach**, the horse lowers his head, stretches out his neck, and adjusts his stride before taking off.
• To **take off**, the horse raises his head and lifts his forelegs off the ground. He brings his hocks up well under his body. He uses his hindquarters to spring forward and upward.

• Now he is in **flight**. He stretches his neck and rounds his back. His forelegs should be tucked right up under him. Once he has cleared the jump with his hind legs, he begins to reach down with his forelegs, ready to land.

• The horse **lands** by straightening his forelegs. His head and neck come up to balance him. The forelegs come down one after the other, then the hind legs.
• The horse is **away** as his hocks come well beneath him so that he recovers his rhythm and balance.

Flight

Take off

Landing

Approach

Away

Jumping position

It is important to make jumping as easy as possible for the horse. He will only be able to give his best if your weight is positioned over his center of motion.
• You can find the correct, balanced position for jumping by moving your weight forward, off the horse's back, as shown on the right.

Your head should be held up so that you look straight ahead.

• It is easier to balance with shorter stirrups. This makes your leg joints bend more than in the normal riding position.
• The lower legs stay straight. They should just touch the horse's sides, so that you can still use them to give commands.
• Knees and ankles carry all your weight. They must remain flexible as they act as shock absorbers.

Your back must be straight, so that you fold forward from the hips, not from your waist. A straight line runs from your elbow to the horse's mouth.

Your heels should point down. If your toes point down you will lose your balance.

Western riding

Western-style riding grew out of the stock and ranching work on the great plains of South America and Midwest U.S.A. It uses long stirrups and reins held in one hand. This makes it useful for many types of ranch work, such as *calf roping**, and competitions such as *barrel racing** and *rodeo riding** which have become very popular. The horses need to be quite small, but tough.

Saddlery

Western saddlery looks different from English *saddlery**. But both are designed for a comfortable fit. Western saddlery varies from simple examples for everyday use, to decorated pieces used in shows.

Parts of a saddle

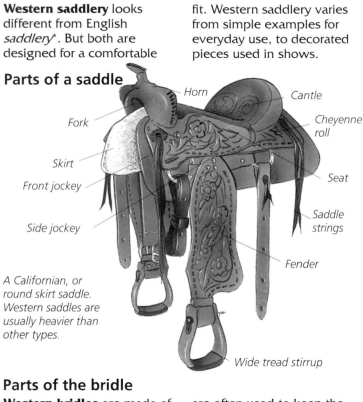

Horn
Cantle
Cheyenne roll
Fork
Skirt
Seat
Front jockey
Saddle strings
Side jockey
Fender
Wide tread stirrup

A Californian, or round skirt saddle. Western saddles are usually heavier than other types.

Parts of the bridle

Western bridles are made of a strong, untanned leather called rawhide. **Browbands** are often used to keep the bridle in place, but *nosebands** are rarely used.
• One type, the **split-ear** or **one-ear bridle**, does not have a browband or a noseband. The headpiece has a split or loop on one side, through which fits the horse's ear. This holds the bridle.

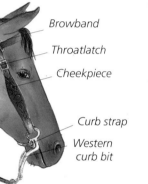

Browband
Throatlatch
Cheekpiece
Curb strap
Western curb bit

Split-ear

Reins

Western reins can be up to 2m (7ft) long. Two types of reins can be used.
• **Split reins** are not joined together at their ends. They pass through the rider's hand, with the forefinger placed between them.

Split reins

• **Californian reins** pass up through the left hand and out between the thumb and forefinger. The ends of Californian reins are held in the rider's right hand on the thigh. They are joined together at their ends with a piece of leather called a **romal**.

Californian reins

Stirrups

Western stirrups are wide and comfortable. They are either made of plain wood or wood bound in leather, or they have a leather tread.

*Barrel racing, 91; Calf roping, 91; Nosebands, 39; Rodeo, 90; Saddlery, 34

For a link to a website where you can read some fascinating facts about Western riding, go to **www.usborne-quicklinks.com**

Mounting

When **mounting**, you should face the near-side (left-hand side) of the horse.

Holding the reins in your left hand, place this hand on the horse's neck just in front of his withers.

Place your left foot in the stirrup in the usual way.

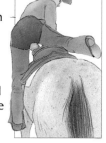

Then, holding the offside swell of the saddle with your right hand, swing your right leg over the horse's back in one smooth movement. You should always keep your leg well clear of the horse's back.

• When **dismounting**, keep the reins in your left hand and place it on the horse's neck. At the same time, hold the saddle horn with your right hand.

Take your right foot out of its stirrup and put your weight into the left stirrup. Then swing your right leg over the horse's back and down to the ground, making sure it is well clear of the horse's back. Take your left foot out of the stirrup.

Position in the saddle

The **Western riding position** is based on balance, with loose reins and little grip. The rider sits deep in the center of the saddle, straight but relaxed. The body should be square to the horse. The legs should be nearly straight, but the rider must not grip the sides of the horse with the knees.

This rider is wearing traditional Western clothes.

Long stirrup leathers allow legs to be straight.

The reins are held lightly in one hand.

Gaits

The comfortable movement of the Western horse, combined with the long stirrups, enables the rider to sit in the saddle at all gaits.

• The **walk** is a four-beat gait which should be smooth and even. The horse should have long, rhythmic strides.

• The **jog** is the same as the *trot** in English riding, except that the Western rider does not rise to the jog. The horse should have even strides.

• The **lope** is a very comfortable three-beat gait, equivalent to a slow *canter** As with the jog, the rider should have a relaxed body but be in complete control.

Turning the horse

In Western riding, the reins are used to turn a horse in a method called **neck reining**. The rein hand is moved in the direction you want to turn.

• To turn to the left, the left hand is taken out to the left side. As the hand moves, the right rein will touch the horse's neck and he will turn away from the pressure.

• This hand movement is combined with the normal *leg aids**. When turning to the left, you should apply pressure with the right leg.

The rider is neck reining to the right.

73

🅱 Dressage

Dressage consists of movements which a horse performs to show the horse and rider in harmony. Dressage is now a popular sport, but originally the movements were used to train *cavalry** horses.

The arena

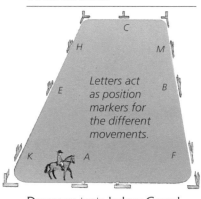

Letters act as position markers for the different movements.

Dressage tests below Grand Prix level are usually done in an arena 40x20m (131x66ft). Grand Prix level uses an arena 60x20m (197x66ft).

Points and penalties

Points are given for each movement: 10 - excellent; 9 - very good; 8 - good; 7 - quite good; 6 - satisfactory; 5 - sufficient; 4 - insufficient; 3 - quite bad; 2 - bad; 1 - very bad; 0 - did not perform.
• **Faults** which will receive a low score: crookedness; incorrect gait; irregularity; loss of rhythm; horse not accepting the bit; loss of balance; loss of *impulsion**; stiff movement; ignoring the rider's *aids**.

Gaits

The **working gait** is the basic dressage gait. In this, the horse "tracks up". This means that his hind feet step into or just over the prints left by the front feet.

In the **collected gait**, the rhythm and tempo are the same as in the working gait, but the horse covers less ground. Steps are shorter, higher and with less speed.

Movements

A **turn on the forehand** is when the hindquarters move around the forelegs, which remain in the same place. The horse must not move forward or backward.
• In the **flying change**, the horse changes *leading legs** during the *canter**. He should spring smoothly from one leading leg to the other.

A flying change

• In the **half pass**, the horse moves diagonally forward and sideways, bent in the direction he is moving.

• A **counter canter** involves cantering while turning right with near-foreleg leading, or cantering and turning left with off-foreleg leading. The horse should be bending towards the leading leg.
• In the **shoulder in**, the horse faces away at an angle of about 30° to the direction of movement. The inside front leg crosses in front of the outside front leg. The toes of hind feet point forward and do not cross over.

The horse looks away from the direction he moves in.

*Aids, 68; Canter, 70; Cavalry, 7; Impulsion, 120; Leading leg, 70

For a link to a website where you can study an animated guide to dressage, go to **www.usborne-quicklinks.com**

The **medium gait** lies between working and extended. The rhythm and tempo remain the same, but the speed increases as the strides cover more ground.

In the **extended pace**, the rhythm and tempo are the same as the medium gait. But each step covers as much ground as possible, increasing the speed.

Pirouette

• A **pirouette** is when the horse's front part circles around his hindquarters, with a radius equal to the length of the horse.
• In the **quarters in**, the horse moves on a three-track basis, the outside hind foot following the track of the inside forefoot. It is usually done at an angle along a wall.
• The **piaffe** is like a *trot** on the spot, with some very *collected**, elevated (raised) steps.

Piaffe

• The **passage** is a slow, very elevated trot, as if the horse is floating above the ground in slow motion. Each step is held suspended in the air for a moment.

Passage

• The **rein back** is when the horse moves backward. Instead of picking up each leg separately as in the forward walk, the horse raises and lowers his legs in diagonal pairs.
• **Leg yielding** is when the horse gives to the pressure of the rider's leg so that his body moves forward and sideways. This is only used in schooling.

*Collected, 118; Trot, 70

Grades of dressage

Competition tests are divided into different levels.
• **Training level** is the simplest and has basic gaits: free walk on long rein, circles of 20m (66ft) diameter at trot and canter. There are **transitions**, or changes of gait, such as trot to halt through a walk.
• **First level** includes circles of 15m (50ft) diameter, and longer strides at trot. The horse walks half circles of 3-5m diameter. From this level onward, transitions become increasingly difficult.
• **2nd - 5th levels**. Circles of 10m (33ft) at trot, medium trot, and extended walk. There are circles of 15m (50ft) at canter, with some counter-canter and medium canter. Includes a collected walk, trot and canter, trot circles of 8m (26ft), counter-canter, a half-pass at trot, and a rein back at walk.
• **Grand Prix** includes trot zig-zags at half-pass, canter with flying changes, half-pirouettes at canter, and four-time flying changes.

Pirouette at canter

▷◁ Show jumping

Show jumping competitions take place in indoor or outdoor arenas. Most competitions have two rounds. The aim of the first round is to complete the course without knocking down any of the jumps. Competitors who do a clear round do a second round, called a jump-off, to decide the winner.

Types of fence

There are two basic types of fences: **verticals** and **oxers**. Vertical fences go straight up and down and are designed to test the horse over heights. Oxers or spread fences are those where the horse has to jump width as well as height. They are all built so that they will fall if knocked. Shaped plastic or metal holders called **cups** are used to hold the fence poles.

6 A **gate** is a vertical jump that is easily knocked as it hangs on flat cups.

7 **Rustic fences** are jumps made of natural materials, such as unpainted wooden poles.

① An **upright rail fence** is a vertical jump, with several poles set directly above one another. This one is difficult, as the horse has little time to judge the height.

③ A **staircase fence**, or **triple bar**, is a spread fence with three rails at graduated heights.

④ A low **cross pole** is the simplest fence to jump. The cross helps the horse or pony to aim for the center.

⑧ A **square oxer** is an oxer with two lines of poles. It is one of the hardest jumps, as the front pole is the same height as the back one.

② A **wall** is a vertical made out of painted wooden blocks and pale top stones. The blocks fall if they are knocked, and some horses find this type of jump *spooky**

⑤ The **hog's back** is a spread jump with the central pole the highest.

⑨ A **fan fence** has three separate poles that fan out from a post at one end, forming a spread jump.

76   *Spooky, 121

For a link to a website where you can take a 360° virtual tour of a show jumping competition and browse an online photo gallery, go to **www.usborne-quicklinks.com**

(10) **Water jumps** are of two types: a water-filled ditch with an upright or spread fence over it; and a much wider jump (shown here), with a wide stretch of water and a low brush fence in front of it. A white tape is placed on the landing side to judge if a horse has faulted.

(10)

• A **combination jump** has two or more obstacles placed close together. Distances between them can be made easier or more difficult, according to the horse's level.

• **Fillers** are different objects, such as brush, straw bales and wooden uprights. They are used to fill up gaps beneath top poles to make them look solid.

Competition rules

Competitors who manage to go clear in the first round, then jump a second round called the **jump-off**.
• The jump-off is usually a shorter course, but it has higher jumps and it is done "against the clock". This means that if two riders have the same number of faults, the one who completes the course in the fastest time wins the competition.

Puissance is a competition which tests the horse's skill at jumping large obstacles.
• There are fewer fences, but they are much larger than in other show jumping classes.

Faults and penalties

• **Running out** is the term used to describe a horse that runs to one side of the fence instead of jumping over it. Penalties are the same as for refusing (see below). Wide fences are more inviting. Riding straight to center of each fence will discourage the horse from running out.

Running out

• A **refusal** is when the horse or pony stops dead and refuses to jump. Three penalty points are given for a first refusal, six for a second refusal, and elimination for a third refusal. Running out may occur through bad

riding, asking the horse to jump too high, or lack of *impulsion**.

Refusal

• **Knocking down** fences is often caused by rushing, or a bad approach. To avoid this, concentrate on rhythm, balance and impulsion. Bright poles and fillers help the horse pay more attention to the jump. Four penalty points are given for a knock down.

*Impulsion, 120

Horse trials

Horse trials are often called **events**. They may be run over one, two or three days. At the most difficult level, three-day events are designed to test the horse and rider in *dressage**, speed and endurance and *show jumping**. Event horses must be at least 5 years old. Most of them are *Thoroughbreds**, which have the right combination of speed and strength.

Dressage

Dressage is the first event.

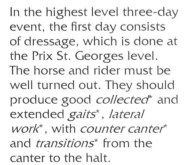

In the highest level three-day event, the first day consists of dressage, which is done at the Prix St. Georges level. The horse and rider must be well turned out. They should produce good *collected** and extended *gaits**, *lateral work**, with *counter canter** and *transitions** from the canter to the halt.

Speed and endurance test

The second day is divided into four phases: A, B, C, and D. These cover a total distance of about 27km (17 miles) in national events, and about 35km (22 miles) in the Olympics.

Roads and tracks
• **Phase A** is a section of roads and tracks, covering 15.2km (9½ miles). This is ridden at alternating steady trot and canter gaits. There are penalties for finishing outside a fixed time.
• **Phase C** (after Phase B) is a another section of roads and tracks, longer than Phase A. It is followed by a 10-minute break, when the horse must be examined by a vet.

Steeplechase
• **Phase B** is a *steeplechase** in which horses must jump 10-12 fences, open ditches, and a water jump. The course can be 1-3km (2miles), and has a fixed time.

Cross-country
• **Phase D** is a **cross-country** course with fixed obstacles designed to test the skills of both horse and rider in a fixed time.
It has 20-32 fences. Many of them are combinations, so the horse might make more than 32 jumps.
The height and spread of the fences changes to present different ways of jumping. Time can be saved by skill and courage.

Show jumping

The final day of the three-day event is a show jumping test. This shows whether, after the tiring second day, the horse is still fit and supple. The obstacles are quite easy, but the course has twists and turns which test both the horse and the rider.

Cross-country fences

Difficult and unusual obstacles test the strength and courage of the horse in the cross-country (Phase D). There are various types, built according to the landscape and local materials.

1 A **palisade** is a simple, inviting-looking fence which can be vertical or slightly sloped to make it more difficult.

2 An **open ditch** is followed by a fence.

3 A **log pile** is a wide stack of logs.

4 A **tiger trap** has rails set at an angle over a ditch, forming an inverted 'V' shape.

5 The **Normandy bank** has a jump up onto a flat bank with a rail on the far edge.

6 A **coffin** has three elements: post and rails followed by a ditch and then another post and rails.

7 A **bullfinch** is a high fence with thick hedge which the horses can jump through the top of.

8 A **stile** is a narrow fence which needs accurate riding. It can cause the horse to run out.

9 The **shark's teeth** is a horizontal bar with "teeth" set against it. The rider aims to jump between the teeth.

10 A **hayrack** is a V-shaped obstacle with a "false" groundline. This can be difficult.

11 The **table** is solid, with heavy, wooden bars. With no clear groundline, it can be difficult to jump.

12 A **step fence** forms the shape of steps going down a hillside.

13 A **drop** fence has the landing side lower than the takeoff.

14 The **bounce** is a fence with two or more obstacles. The horse jumps (bounces) over each without a stride in between.

15 **Water jumps** vary. The horse may have to jump over the water, or over a fence into it. There may also be a fence in the water to jump over. Water jumps often cause refusals or falls.

79

Gymkhanas

Gymkhanas are riding competitions which involve races and mounted games. They were introduced to Britain by soldiers returning from India, where games on horseback had been played for centuries. They are very popular in Britain, especially with children and ponies.

Prince Philip Cup

The **Prince Philip Cup**, sponsored by the Washington International Horse Show in October, determines the top Junior Games team in the U.S. Teams qualify by competing at the Pony Club's National Championships.

Races

There are a number of different races designed to try both the rider's and the pony's agility and skill.
• In **speed games**, the rider has to get from one end of the arena to the other and back again as quickly as possible.
• In **precision games**, the rider has to pick up an object, carry it, or balance it on another object.

Flag race

The flag race tests the horse's ability to turn at speed.

In the **flag race**, a flag on a pole is picked up at one end of the arena and dropped into a holder at the far end.

Apple bobbing

In **apple bobbing**, the rider gallops to a bucket, dismounts and tries to catch an apple inside the bucket with his teeth. The apple is floating in water, which makes it more difficult. Apple in mouth, the rider mounts the pony and gallops back.

Bending

Competitors must not knock over any of the poles.

Bending is one of the most popular races for all age groups. It is also one of the fastest. Each rider has to bend, or ride, in and out of a line of six poles, go around the end one, and come back again as fast as possible.

What to wear

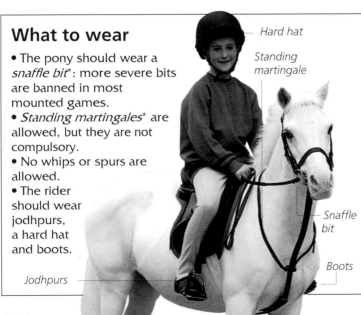

• The pony should wear a *snaffle bit**: more severe bits are banned in most mounted games.
• *Standing martingales** are allowed, but they are not compulsory.
• No whips or spurs are allowed.
• The rider should wear jodhpurs, a hard hat and boots.

Hard hat

Standing martingale

Snaffle bit

Boots

Jodhpurs

*Martingale, 41; Snaffle bit, 40

For a link to a website where you can take part in some fun pony games, go to **www.usborne-quicklinks.com**

Egg and spoon

The **egg and spoon race** requires a lot of concentration. The rider gallops to the end of the arena to get the egg, dismounts, then runs back beside the pony, still carrying the egg in the spoon.

Potato race

In the **potato race**, each competitor has to collect potatoes, one at a time, and drop them in a bucket near the start. If he drops one, he has to dismount, pick it up, remount and continue.

If the rider is close to the bucket, the potato should not bounce out.

Carton race

In the **carton race**, ice cream (or other) cartons have to be built up to form a tower. This requires precision and care and can be difficult unless the pony is under control.

Sack race

In the **sack race**, a line of sacks is laid on the ground. The rider gallops up to the line, stops quickly and dismounts. He gets into a sack and jumps or shuffles his way to the finish.

Walk, trot and canter

Riders have to walk up the arena, then trot and canter back. If the pony breaks into a faster gait than the one he is supposed to be doing, the competitor has to turn a circle before continuing in the correct gait.

Musical sacks

In **musical sacks**, sacks are placed on the ground and all the competitors ride around the outside track. Each time the music stops, they try to find a sack, jump off their ponies and stand on the sack. There are not enough sacks for everyone, since some are removed each time.

Musical sacks

The winner of the musical sacks is the rider who reaches the last remaining sack, dismounts and then stands on it before the other rider.

Vaulting on

Vaulting on is the act of springing or vaulting from the ground onto the pony's back. It can be done while the pony is moving forward at a fast trot or slow canter. This helps to speed up the rider's performance in the race. It can be difficult to learn and requires skill and agility. Timing is important.

Showing

In a **showing** competition, horses and ponies are judged mainly on how they look, behave and move. The competition is divided into different classes, organized according to the type, breed, size and age of the animal.

How the horses are shown

When horses or ponies are shown **in hand**, they are led around the ring at a walk, while the judges watch from the center. They are then lined up, inspected individually and trotted up.

As well as looking good, the horses and ponies in ridden classes must go well **under saddle** at all *gaits**. They must also be a good ride. To test this, judges sometimes ride the horses.

Family pony

Different classes

• A **show hunter** is judged on his suitability for riding to hounds, although he will probably never hunt.
• There is also a class of **show hunter pony** (shown below).

• The **working hunter** is similar to a show hunter. But this class is judged half on jumping performance over a short course, and half as for the show hunter class.

Cob

• A **cob** should be between 14.2 h.h. and 15.1 h.h. The heavyweight category must be able to carry over 14 stone. He must be well-built.

• A **hack** is smaller and more elegant than a hunter. His conformation must be excellent and he must also be a comfortable ride. There are large hacks (standing up to 15.3 h.h.), small hacks (between 14.2 h.h. and 15 h.h.), and ladies' hacks which are to be ridden *sidesaddle**.

Ladies' hack

• **Mountain and moorland** classes are for pure-bred *British pony breeds**. Judges look for a pony that is beautiful, as well as being strong and well-built, and typical of his class, showing hardiness and good sense.

Mountain and moorland

• The **family horse and pony** class is judged on how he performs when ridden, rather than on looks. He may have to jump, and should be suitable for all members of a family to ride.
• The **show pony** is divided into height classes: up to 14.2 h.h.; up to 13.2 h.h.; and up to 12.2 h.h. Each is ridden by children of different age groups. Show ponies are very beautiful and of a finer build than other types.

Show pony

• A **riding horse** covers any *mare** or *gelding** over 15 h.h., not entitled to show in the hack, hunter or cob classes. *Conformation** should give a smooth and comfortable ride.

*British pony breeds, 26; Conformation, 16; Gaits, 70; Gelding, 15; Mare, 15; Sidesaddle, 69

Ringcraft

• Once the riders have gone around the ring in a group, they line up and each does an **individual show** alone. The horse is put through his gaits, with transitions and cantered on each lead.

• **Stripping off** is when the horses and ponies are individually inspected by the judge. The rider dismounts and the saddle is removed and placed out of the way on the ground.

Riders and their horses line up for the individual show.

• The **halt**, or **showing a leg**, is when each horse is led out and halts for the judge to assess conformation.

He stands so that the judge can see all four legs in profile. Some U.S. breed classes show their pairs of legs close together.

• With **trotting up**, the horse is walked away and trotted past the judge to assess the action. He looks at movement, straightness, and for faults such as *paddling**.

Performance

A horse or pony for showing should be obedient and completely under the rider's control.

• He must be light on his *forehand**, carrying his weight on his hindquarters rather than the forelegs.
• He must have good balance.
• He has to be on the bit, accepting the rider's contact.
• His rhythm must be good, with regular, even steps.
• His *extension** must be good, lengthening his stride and using lots of *impulsion**.

Turnout

Trimming

Many horses and ponies are quite hairy and look much better if they are trimmed before showing. But some breeds, such as native ponies, should never be trimmed or braided, as they are shown in their natural state.

• The beard (on the jaw and throat) should be trimmed with scissors at an upward slant.

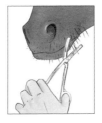

• On the ears, only those hairs sticking out should be trimmed.
• The mane should never be cut with scissors. But a section can be cut behind the ears, so that the headpiece sits comfortably.
• The tail should be trimmed so that it hangs 8-10cm (3-4in) below the hocks.

Braiding

Braiding the mane and tail helps the horse look nice. The number and placing of the braids can help make the neck conformation look better.

The horse's head and neck are very important features, and braiding helps to show them off clearly.

Braided mane

Racing

Horse racing is one of the oldest of all sports. It featured in the Olympic Games of ancient Greece. There are several types of races today. A **racehorse** is a horse which has been specially bred for racing. The *Thoroughbred** is the most famous breed.

Flat racing

A **flat race** is run over a course with no obstacles. The most famous flat races run in the U.S. are the Kentucky Derby, run at Churchill Downs in Kentucky; the Preakness, run at Pimlico Park in Maryland; and the Belmont, run at Belmont Park in New York. These races make up the Triple Crown.

Steeplechases

A **steeplechase** is a race in which the horses have to jump fences, ditches and a water jump.
• The first steeplechase was run in Ireland in 1752. The most famous British race is the **Grand National**. The biggest European race is the Czech **Grand Pardubice**, which was founded in 1874.

Horses jumping a steeplechase fence

Point-to-points

Point-to-point is a form of steeplechasing for *hunters**. Point-to-points were first run across country, from one point to another.
  Competitors must have a certificate stating that each horse has been regularly hunted with a pack of hounds. Races are open to amateur riders only, both men and women.

Hurdling

In a **hurdle race** there must be at least eight hurdles on a course, at least 3.2 km (2 miles) long. For every extra 0.4 km (¼ mile), there should be one more hurdle. The hurdles are smaller than those in steeplechases.
• The first recorded hurdle race was held near Bristol, in England in 1821.
• The most important one is the **Champion Hurdle** at Cheltenham, England.

Harness racing

Horse pulling a sulky

In **harness**, or **trotting racing**, horses pull riders in light vehicles called **sulkies**, or *gigs**, at the *trot**. Harness racing is very popular in the U.S.A. Races are usually run over 1.6 km (1 mile), which can be covered in 1.54 minutes.
  The American Standardbred is one of the best horses for trotting.

Palio

The **Palio** of Siena in Italy was first run in 1482. The course is around the main city square. Riders represent different districts of the city. The race is named after the painted silk banner, or palio, awarded to the winner. A

large procession is held before the race, with everyone dressed in colorful clothes.

Starting stalls and gates

• **Starting stalls** are the sets of stalls which hold the horses at the starting line of a race. The gates at the front of the stalls open to release the horses.

• A **starting gate** is a barrier used at the start of a race. Lines of tapes are stretched across the course to posts on each side. They fly up when the starter releases a catch.

Jockeys

A **jockey** is any rider who competes in a horse race. Many professional jockeys begin by becoming apprentices with a trainer or racing horse owner. In addition to being a good rider, a jockey must also be small and light.

• Requirements vary from state to state, but jockeys must generally be under 59kg (130 lbs).

• The **racing seat** is the special position adopted for flat racing. *Stirrup leathers** are short and the jockey sits forward and clear of the saddle. Steeplechase jockeys usually sit farther back in the saddle, with longer stirrup leathers.

Weighing-out and weighing-in

All horses must carry a certain weight in races, depending on the race conditions or the weight allowed by an official called the **handicapper**. In flat racing the minimum weight is 44kg (98lb), while for steeplechase and hurdle races it is 63.5kg (140lb).

• Each jockey is weighed for the horse he is about to ride. This takes place at least 15 minutes before the start of the race. This is known as **weighing-out**.

• At the end of the race, every jockey must be weighed again. This is called **weighing-in**.

• A **handicap** in a race is when the weights to be carried by the horses are adjusted by the handicapper. The purpose of this is to equalize the horses' chances of winning.

Silks

Silks are the racing colors worn in flat racing and in steeplechasing, on the jockey's jacket and cap to indicate the horse's owner. Different colors and patterns can be combined. The colors are registered by the owners. A jockey must change his silks for each owner he rides for.

Racing silks

*Gig, 95; Hunter, 82; Stirrup leathers, 37; Thoroughbred, 31; Trot, 70

Long-distance riding is a form of competition riding. It began in Australia and the U.S.A. and then became popular in Europe. There are three levels. The easiest is the non-competitive pleasure ride. The endurance ride is the most difficult.

Trail and endurance rides have maximum time limits.

Pleasure rides

Pleasure rides are non-competitive and take the form of organized groups of riders with a leader. They are between 23 km (15 miles) and 46 km (30 miles) long, and can last just a few hours or a whole day.
• Pleasure rides are popular on ranches and state parks, on moorland and downland, and through forests.
• Riders of all levels of experience can take part. Any type of horse will do, but he must be experienced, sensible and well-mannered.

Pleasure rides can be gentle rides through beautiful countryside.

Trail rides

Trail rides are competitive cross-country rides which are very popular in North America. Distances vary widely, from 40 km in one day up to 160 km (100 miles) over three days. In Britain, they range from 40 km (25 miles) to 96 km (60 miles) in one day.
• The annual **Vermont One Hundred Mile Three-Day Trail Ride** is one of the best-known in the U.S.A.

Endurance rides

The **endurance ride** is the most difficult level of long-distance riding. It has become very popular in many countries and the basic rules in each country are similar. There is a maximum time limit for the ride, but no minimum limit.
• The U.S.A. is the leading country at this level. There are over thirty 80-160 km (50-100 miles) endurance rides in the U.S.A., with 50 to 200 competitors in each.
• In Britain and other countries, distances are from 80 km (50 miles) to 160 km (100 miles) in one day.

Veterinary checks

Vets carry out strict checks on horses before, during and after trail and endurance rides.

The vet makes a thorough check before the horse can continue.

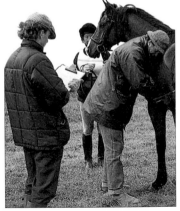

• A horse is checked all over before the ride starts. The rider will receive a certificate to ride only if the horse is fit to take part.
• There are more veterinary checks at regular points along the route.
• The horse is checked again after completing a long-distance ride. The vet checks that the horse is in a good condition, and that the pulse and breathing rates are back to normal.

 # Polo

Polo is a ball game played on horseback. It is played at a gallop and is the fastest team game in the world. The earliest record of it dates back to 525BC, when it was played in Persia and India. Now it is played in many parts of the world, especially in Argentina, which has become the leading polo country.

Polo pony

A **polo pony** is a mixture of different horse breeds. Argentinian-bred ponies - the native Criollos crossed with *Thoroughbreds** - make the best polo ponies.
• Polo ponies can be of any height, but the ideal is about 15.1 h.h. They should be fast, strong and brave, and have good balance.

Polo rules are very strict, but players can "ride off" (force out) opposing team members.

Players wear protective helmets.

Knee guards

Boots or bandages protect legs.

The equipment

The **polo stick**, known as a **mallet** in the U.S.A., has a flexible handle made of cane or bamboo 120-137cm (48-54ins) long. At the end of the handle is a wooden head set at right angles. This is made of sycamore, ash or bamboo.
• The **polo ball** is made of willow wood or bamboo root. It is quite small, measuring 8cm (3ins) in diameter.

The game

A polo game is played by two teams of four players, each of whom has a handicap. Players try to hit the ball between the opponents' goalposts to score a goal. There are usually two mounted **umpires**.

Gloves help give a good grip on the polo stick.

• There are goal posts at each end of the polo field. They must be at least 3m (10ft) high, and set 7.3m (24ft) apart. The polo field measures a maximum 274m (300 yds) long by 180m (200 yds) wide.
• A **handicap** in a game is the name given to the advantages which some players are given over others. This helps to equalize their chances of winning. The best polo players are given the highest handicap. The handicaps of each player in a team are added together. The lower total number is then subtracted from the higher total number of the opposing team. This gives the number of advantage goals which is allowed to the team with the lower handicap.
• A **chukka** is the term used for the periods into which a polo game is divided. One chukka lasts seven minutes. Because it is such a fast game, each pony is allowed to play only two chukkas, so each player uses a number of ponies.

Tails are bound for protection.

For a link to a website where you can browse polo photo galleries and read a brief history of polo, go to **www.usborne-quicklinks.com**   *Thoroughbred, 31*

Ball games

There are a number of different ball games played on horseback. Polocrosse was played in Japan over 1,000 years ago, but is now a very popular game in Australia. Buzkashi is still played in Afghanistan where it may have originated 700 years ago. Horseball is a new game, which originated in France.

Buzkashi

Buzkashi is a simple but energetic form of rugby played on horseback. The name derives from the Afghan words *buz*, meaning "goat", and *kashidant*, meaning "to pull". It is also sometimes called **Dragging the Goat**, because the ball is a stuffed goatskin.

• Buzkashi is played by teams, each of which can have more than 25 players, so there may be over 100 players in one game.
  The best riders are called **chapandaz**. They are hired by the owners of the horses. Buzkashi horses have no limit to their height, but they must be strong and fast.

Polocrosse

Polocrosse is a combination of *polo** and another ball game called lacrosse. It was introduced to Europe in the 1930s when it was played on an indoor court. Now it is played on an outdoor field.

Polocrosse stick and ball

• A **polocrosse ball** is made of white, thick-skinned rubber.
• The **polocrosse stick** consists of a cane polo stick shaft, 1-1.2m (4ft) long, with a squash racket head. This has a linen or nylon net in which the ball is carried.

• There are two teams with six players each. They are divided into two groups with three players in each group. They play alternate *chukkas** of eight minutes each. The No.1 (Attack) is the only player who can score a goal. The No.2 (Center) can only play in the center area, while No.3 (Defense) is the only one who is allowed to defend a goal.
• The Australian stock horse is usually used in polocrosse. The ideal height should be no more than 15.2 h.h. Unlike polo, each player is allowed only one horse.

A polocrosse ball being thrown to another player

• A **polocrosse field** is 146.5m (481ft) long and 55m (180ft) wide. There are goal posts 2.5m (8ft) apart at each end.

Penalty line *Center field*

There is a line across the field called the **penalty line**. This encloses the goal-scoring area which only the No.1 player of the attacking team and the No.3 player of the defending team can enter.
  The game begins with the ball being thrown in by the umpire. Players gallop with it or throw it from player to player, until the No.1 is in a position to throw a goal. The total number of goals scored by the two groups in each team gives the final score.

*Chukka, 87; Polo, 87

For a link to a website where you can find out the answers to frequently asked questions about polocrosse, go to **www.usborne-quicklinks.com**

• The rough ground where the game is played, called a **maidan**, is unlimited in size. Two goal posts lie about 0.8 km (½ mile) apart. Around each goal post is drawn a circle about 46 m (50 yds) across.

• The game can last several hours. It starts with the ball being thrown into the scrum of players, as in rugby. The goal is to pick it off the ground without dismounting, tuck it under the knee, and then gallop round the far goal post and back to the circle.

• A successful run around the goal post earns the player and his team one point and prize money. Umpires award points after each goal, and decide which team has won.

Horseball

Horseball is a cross between rugby and basketball, played on horseback. At the top level the game is played mostly at the canter or gallop.

• The ball is of a small size, held in a special harness with six leather handles attached.

• The match consists of two halves of 10 minutes each, with a half time of three minutes.

• The game starts with one of the teams picking up the ball from the center of the field at a canter. They pass it to each other as they race toward the goal. A team must make at least three passes, forward or backward, between three different players without dropping the ball before a goal can be scored. A player must not keep the ball more than 10 seconds.

Area of play

Security zone

• The game is played on a fairly small field, roughly 70m (77ft) long and 30m (33ft) wide. There is a goal post at each end. This consists of a metal hoop, 1m (3½ft) in diameter which is suspended on a pole 3.5m (11½ft) above ground.

• There are two teams of six players each. Only four players are on the field at the same time. The other two are substitutes.

Catching the ball in a horseball match

A player holds up his hand hoping to intercept the ball from the opposition.

Rodeo

The name **rodeo** comes from the Spanish for "round-up", because a rodeo was originally a round-up of cattle. Today the word is mainly used to describe special shows held in front of large audiences, in which riders demonstrate their skills. Most contestants are professional rodeo riders, rather than *cowboys** or stockmen, and they can win large prizes.

Pole bending

One of the rodeo events is **pole bending**. Each rider has to bend, or ride in and out of, a line of poles, without knocking any of them down. He rides around the end pole and back again.

Bucking broncos

Bronco is the name originally given to the wildest, untamable Mustang horses of America. A **bucking bronco** is now usually an untamed cross-breed, such as a *Thoroughbred** crossed with *Clydesdale**. A bronco may be easy to handle but as soon as a rider is sitting on his back he will try to throw him off by kicking and bucking (jumping vertically with straight legs and arched back). Testing a rider's skill on an unbroken horse is known as **bronc riding**.

Saddle bronc riding

The saddle used in **saddle bronc riding** is a small *Western saddle**, without a horn. The rein is a rope tied to the horse's halter. A bucking strap is tied around the horse's loins to encourage him to buck.

When the rider is sitting in the saddle, a gate is opened to let horse and rider into the arena.

At that moment the horse bucks out into the ring, throwing the rider around.

The ride must last ten seconds and the rider needs very good balance and timing for the best score.

He must use only one hand. He will be disqualified if he touches the horse with his free hand, changes hands on the rein, or is thrown before the ten seconds is complete.

Saddle bronc riding

Belt with handle

Bareback bronc riding

Bareback bronc riding

Bareback bronc riding often produces some of the wildest riding at the rodeo.

The rider has no saddle. He holds onto the horse with one hand only, holding a handle attached to a strap around the horse's belly.

Rules and scoring are similar to saddle bronc riding, except that the time limit is eight seconds, not ten.

*Clydesdale, 32; Cowboy, 100; Thoroughbred, 31; Western saddle, 72

For a link to a website where you can try out a rodeo quiz, go to **www.usborne-quicklinks.com**

Cutting

Cutting is one of the most popular events with both the riders and spectators. This involves horse and rider separating a steer (young castrated bull) from the rest of a herd within a set time. It must also be prevented from rejoining the herd.

Although both horse and rider take part, it is the horse's natural ability which is tested. He must be very careful not to disturb or scatter the rest of the herd when separating the steer.

Barrel racing

Barrel racing is the only women's event in rodeo. Competitors race between and around three large oil drums, placed to form a triangular course. The rider gallops to the first barrel, goes around it, gallops to the next, and then on to the third in a clover leaf pattern. She then returns to the starting line. The winner is the rider with the fastest time.

Barrel racing between oil drums

Steer wrestling

The **steer wrestling** contest has to use very well-trained horses. The competition begins when a steer is let loose into the arena. The cowboy gallops after it. Another rider, called a **hazer**, races on the other side, to keep the animal running straight through the arena.

Steer wrestling

When the cowboy draws level with the steer's head, he throws himself from the saddle, catches hold of the steer's head and horns, and tries to wrestle the animal down onto its side.

Calf roping

A **calf roping** contest involves roping and tying a calf, as if to prepare it for branding. This requires skill with a *lasso***** and a well-trained horse.

A calf is released into the arena and the horse and rider gallop after it. Then the cowboy throws his lasso over the animal's head and ties the other end of the rope around his saddle horn. He jumps off his horse and runs toward the calf.

Once he has caught the calf, the cowboy ties three of its legs together with a short rope, called a **piggin' string**.

Chuckwagon racing

Chuckwagon racing is one of the most colorful of all the rodeo events.
• A **chuckwagon** is a four-wheeled wooden wagon with a canvas hood, as once used on cattle roundups. The wagons are stripped down for lightness. Teams of four horses pull each one. Collisions and overturned wagons make these races very exciting.

*Lasso, 120

Driving

Horses were probably used for driving, or pulling chariots, before they were used for riding. The modern sport of driving dates from the late 18th century. Driving competitions test the all-around skills of both drivers and horses.

Stages in training

Long reining

The first stage in training is when a horse is taught driving movements by a trainer on foot. This is called **long reining**.

The goal is to teach the horse to respond to *hand aids** and voice commands, to make him more supple by practicing turns, and to improve *impulsion**.

The trainer should be just close enough for control.

Two reins are used for long reining. The trainer walks behind and to one side of the horse. He keeps a light contact with the horse's mouth through the reins. He is able to move the horse in different directions, with control over the *gait**.

Breaking in

The next stage is to get the horse used to wearing a harness, and to the feel and noise of pulling a light weight. This is called **breaking in**. Sometimes he pulls a log or tire over different surfaces such as grass or gravel.

• **Long lines** are attached to the collar on each side of the horse, and to the object being pulled. These can be released quickly if the horse panics.

Putting to

When a horse is harnessed to a vehicle it is called **putting to**.

For a single harness, the vehicle is brought to the horse with shafts raised above the quarters. The shafts are then lowered and passed through the tugs.

The traces are then fastened to trace hooks on the vehicle, their length is adjusted, and they are pulled tight.

The harness

The main parts of a **driving harness** are the *bridle**, the collar and traces, the pad or saddle (to support the shafts) and the breeching.

1 The **headpiece** is the part of the bridle to which the cheekpieces, throat latch and browband are fixed.

2 The **throat latch** is a buckled strap which prevents the bridle from slipping over the ears.

3 The **browband** is a leather strap which is fixed to the top of the bridle. It prevents the bridle from slipping back on the neck.

4 The **cheekpiece** is the part of the bridle to which the *bit** is attached. Blinkers and the noseband are also attached to it, if used.

5 A **Liverpool bit** is the usual bit for driving. Two or three slots on the bar make it more or less severe, so giving the rider varying control of the horse.

6 A **noseband** is a leather band attached to the cheekpieces. It is slotted through them.

*Bits, 40; Bridle, 38; Gaits, 70; Hand aids, 68; Impulsion, 120

For a link to a website where you can find out a lot more about horse driving trials, go to **www.usborne-quicklinks.com**

(7) **Blinkers** are eye blinds on the cheekpieces, which block views to side and rear which might frighten the horse.

(8) The **collar** is made of padded leather and fits around the horse's neck. It is designed to carry the hames. Sometimes a **breast collar** is used instead.

Neck collar (left) and breast collar

(9) **Hames** are made of steel. The traces are attached to them.

(12) The **backband** is a strap running through the driving pad. It carries the weight of the shafts or traces.

(13) The **bellyband** attaches to the backband. It helps to stabilize the backband and to keep the shafts in position on either side of the horse.

(14) The **crupper** is a leather loop used to hold the driving saddle or pad in place and stop it moving forward.

(15) The **breeching** is a thick leather band around the horse's quarters, which carries the weight of the vehicle when moving down hills or backing.

(17) **Traces** are the thick leather straps used to harness the horse to the vehicle.

(18) **Shafts** are the bars between which the horse is harnessed to a single-horse vehicle.

(19) **Tugs** are leather loops on either side which connect the shafts to the backband.

(20) **Driving reins** are put on the horse last. They are buckled to the bit in the usual way.

*A **driving whip** is only used to help the driver to direct the horse.*

(10) A **driving saddle** is worn by single horses. A **driving pad** is lighter than a saddle and is used with two horses, called a *pair**.

(11) **Terrets** are the two rings attached to the pad through which the driving reins are passed.

(16) The **girth** is used to secure the saddle or pad on the back of the horse.

*Pair, 94

Harness formations

There are various different **formations** in driving, each of them using a different number of horses.

• The **leader** is a driven horse which leads another. There are sometimes two leading horses at the front of a team, one called the **near leader** and the other the **off leader**.

• The **wheeler** is the name given to the horse or team of horses nearest to the vehicle they are pulling, as opposed to the leaders of the team.

• In **single harness** driving, one horse is driven alone. Lighter, two- or four-wheeled vehicles are used.

• In a **pair**, two horses are driven abreast, one beside the other. Light two-wheel or larger four-wheel vehicles are used in this type of formation.

A pair pulling a four-wheeled vehicle

• A **tandem** consists of two horses, one driven in front of the other. They pull two- or four-wheel vehicles.

A tandem

This carriage is being pulled by a four-in-hand. The driver controls the horses with long reins.

The traces are buckled to the horses' collars.

The leaders' traces are attached to this wooden bar.

Blinkers prevent the horses from seeing to the side and behind, so that they are not alarmed.

Wheelers

Leaders

For a link to a website where you can take an online tour of an amazing collection of carriages, go to **www.usborne-quicklinks.com**

- A **troika** is a Russian term for a team of three horses driven abreast, usually with a carriage called a caleche.

A troika

- A **unicorn** is a team of three horses, with two wheelers and one leader in front.
- A **four-in-hand** is a team of four horses with two wheelers and two leaders. A coach pulled by a four-in-hand is sometimes known as a **complete turn-out**. Because of the number of horses, heavier four-wheel vehicles are used.

Horse-drawn vehicles

The earliest surviving carriage is the chariot of the Egyptian pharaoh Tutankhamun (1361-1352BC), now in the Cairo Museum. In Europe, the great age of horse-drawn vehicles was in the 18th and 19th centuries.

Governess carts

The **governess cart** is a light and low two-wheeled trap for one horse or pony. It is also known as a tub-cart or car, and seats four passengers facing each other. It is entered through a back door.

A governess cart

Gigs

The **gig** is a two-wheeled carriage which carries two people only. There are many variations.

A gig

- A **Lawton gig** is a stylish, well-sprung gig.
- The **Liverpool gig** is similar to the Lawton.
- The **Stanhope gig** has a seat resting on the boot.
- The **Murrieta gig** has a folding hood.
- The **Tilbury gig** is supported at the back by three upright rails.

Phaetons

A **phaeton** is a four-wheeled carriage. There are many different versions.
- A **Park phaeton** is a low-hung phaeton for a lady's use. It is also known as a **George IV's**, **Lady's**, or **Peter's phaeton**.

A phaeton

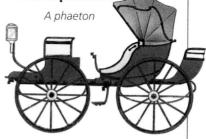

- The **Mail phaeton** is the heaviest type of phaeton for a pair of horses. It is built in a similar way to a *mail coach**.
- The **Demi-mail phaeton** is a lighter and more elegant form of mail phaeton. It was used in town and country.
- The **Spider phaeton** is the lightest of all the phaetons, pulled by a single horse or a pair.

Landaus

The **Landau** is an open carriage, equipped with an adjustable leather hood. It was designed at Landau in Germany in 1757.

A Landau

Driving trials

Carriage driving competitions, known as **driving trials**, have become very popular in Europe and North America. They are based on the ridden *three-day event**. A competition opens with presentation, followed by dressage, the marathon, and finally the obstacle driving.

Presentation

During the **presentation**, the judges consider the appearance and condition of the horses, the drivers and their vehicles. They award points out of 10.

Dressage

In the **dressage** phase, the tests include changes of *gait** and direction. Competitors are judged on their accuracy, precision and correctness of the gaits. The following gaits are included in the dressage phase of the competition.
• The **walk** must be brisk, with good rhythm.
• In the **working trot**, the horses should move with even, elastic steps and good action in the *hocks**.
• In the **collected trot**, the horse's steps are shorter. But his action is lighter and more mobile than in the working trot. The neck is raised.
• In the **extended trot**, the horse lengthens his stride and extends his neck. This produces greater *impulsion** from the hindquarters.

Marathon

The **marathon** includes numerous natural and artificial obstacles known as **hazards**, such as hills, water, trees and gates. More penalty points can be collected in this part than in the other three parts together. In international events, competitors have to cover distances of between 23-27km (37-43 miles). The final section is the most challenging, including 5-8 hazards done to a time limit.

A four-in-hand crosses a water hazard on the marathon course.

Obstacle driving

Obstacle driving consists of driving around a course of pairs of cones with balls placed on top. The vehicle used must be the same one used in the dressage phase.
• Faults include: knocking over a cone or dislodging a ball; the *groom** dismounting; disobedience from the horses; knocking over the start or finish flags.

A team negotiates the obstacle course.

*Gaits, 70; Groom, 119; Hock, 10; Impulsion, 120; Three-day event, 78

Vaulting

Vaulting involves gymnastics on the back of a moving horse. It was used by the Romans as part of their basic riding lessons, and also to train knights in Medieval Europe. Vaulting has now become a popular sport.

Vaulting equipment

The **vaulting surcingle** has two handles or grips for the vaulter to hold. A ring on top helps with exercises, such as kneeling and standing on the horse's back. Two loops for the feet are sometimes fitted on the sides.

Foot loop

Exercises

A competition team has eight members, and each must perform six basic exercises. They are given scores of 0-10, based on form, grace and precision.

• The **basic seat** should have the upper body straight, with the weight spread equally on both seat bones. Both legs are held against the horse's sides.

• In the **flare**, the right leg is lifted backward and straightened. The left arm is stretched out in front.

Flare

• **Standing** begins when the vaulter goes from sitting to kneeling. He or she slowly straightens up into a vertical position with arms out.

Standing

• The **mill** is a four-step exercise. The vaulter moves around from facing forward, into an inward-facing position. He or she then moves to face backward, and then outward. Finally, they return to the forward seat again.

Mill

• In the **flank**, or **half scissors**, both legs are swung backward to meet in the air.

Flank

The vaulter then sits in an inward-facing position, with the legs stretched out. He or she swings the legs up into the air and lands on the ground.

• In the **scissors** the vaulter swings both legs backward into the air. The left leg is crossed over the right leg and the vaulter lands in the rear-facing sitting position. The legs are swung forward. The vaulter returns to face forward and finally vaults off.

Scissors

A team of three vaulters performing more advanced exercises

For a link to a website where you can look at amazing photos of gymnasts on horseback, go to **www.usborne-quicklinks.com**

Performing horses

Horses have been entertaining people ever since the chariot races of the Roman Empire. They still dazzle audiences with their skill, grace and beauty, in classical riding schools and circuses, and in films and on television.

The Spanish Riding School

The Spanish Riding School of Vienna is the oldest riding school in the world. *Lipizzaners** demonstrate classical equitation, based on 16th- and 17th-century riding skills.

Airs above the ground

The horses perform a series of movements called **airs above the ground**. These are based on the jumps and kicks made by medieval warhorses in battle to keep away enemy foot soldiers.

• The **levade** involves the horse rising up on his hind legs. He then draws his forelegs in, while the hindquarters carry his body weight.

Levade

• In the **courbette**, the horse rears up, jumps forward off his hocks and lands again with hocks bent. He moves forward in short leaps.

Courbette

• In the **capriole**, the horse makes a half-rear, with the hocks drawn under him, then jumps forward and high up in the air. He kicks his hind legs out and lands on all four legs.

Capriole

• In the **ballotade**, the horse leaps up so that he is almost parallel to the ground. The forelegs are bent at the knees, hind legs showing their shoes. But the legs are not stretched out as they would be in kicking.

Ballotade

• The **croupade** is similar to the ballotade, except that the horse does not show its shoes.

Circus horses

A rosinback with a performing juggler

Animals are not used in circuses as much as they once were. But some circuses still have highly trained performing horses.

Rosinbacks

The **rosinback**, or **jockey horse**, is a broad-backed horse which canters around the ring while riders perform acrobatic acts on his back. The name derives from the resin (rosin) that is rubbed into the horse's back to prevent the performers from slipping.

Liberty horses

Liberty horses perform a series of movements in groups of about 12. They are unridden and controlled only by a trainer or presenter who stands on the ground.

*Arabs** are often used because of their beauty and courage, and because they are not too large.

*Arab, 28; Lipizzaner, 31

For a link to a website where you can watch some exciting video clips of Lipizzaners demonstrating 'airs above the ground' and other movements, go to **www.usborne-quicklinks.com**

High School

The Spanish walk

High School is a form of *classical equitation**. A High School horse is trained to perform movements such as the levade. *Thoroughbreds** are often trained in this way.

• The **Spanish walk** is a movement in which the horse lifts his forelegs very high, and extends them straight out. It is popular in the circus, but not in classical High School.

Film and TV horses

The cinema and television rely heavily on performing horses. Many famous stories would be impossible to show on the screen without a horse. There have been many legendary scenes of horses in films such as *Ben Hur*.

TV star Roy Rogers and his horse

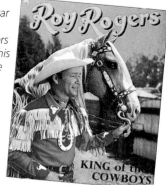

Famous performers

• **Philip Astley** (1742-1814) was the creator of the modern circus. He was a soldier in the British army. At the age of 24 he left the army and, with his horse Gibraltar, started his first circus which was held in a field in London.

His circus, known as **Astley's Amphitheatre**, became very popular and staged daring feats of horsemanship. The circus toured Europe as far east as Belgrade. Similar circuses were soon formed throughout Europe.

• **William Frederick Cody** (1846-1917), known as **Buffalo Bill**, was a U.S. scout and performer. From 1883, he toured the US and Europe with an exciting **Wild West Show**. This featured realistic re-creations of attacks by Native Americans.

For a time his team also included the sharpshooter **Annie Oakley**, and **Chief Sitting Bull**, who defeated Custer's troops at the Battle of Little Big Horn in 1876.

Tricks and stunts

Horses used in films and television are often ridden by **stunt riders**, who give incredible demonstrations of their riding skills.

The horses have often been trained to do particular tricks. For example, some are trained to fall over at the squeeze of the rider's leg.

In Western films, Native American horses such as the Pinto are used to fit in with the story.

*Classical equitation, 118; Thoroughbred, 31

Working horses

For at least 6,000 years, until the introduction of the car in the early 20th century, horses played a vital role as a means of transportation and for work. In some countries they still play a part in people's lives.

Plowing

Horses have only been used comparatively recently in the cultivation of land. They were originally considered too valuable for that sort of work.

In the Middle East and Asia, donkeys and oxen have always been used for plowing the soil and for pulling carts.

Heavy horses plowing a field

Centuries later, people discovered the strength and intelligence of the *heavy horses**, and they replaced oxen for work. But with the invention of the *steam engine**, the use of heavy horses declined, as they were replaced by machinery.

In some parts of the world, in the vineyards of France for example, horses are still used for some farm work.

Ranching

In North and South America and Australia, horses are still used to round up cattle. The cowhands ride particular types of horses for this work.

A cowboy on a cutting horse rounds up a steer.

- In North America, the cowhands are known as **cowboys**. A cowboy is a man who works on the big cattle ranches to guard and round up cattle which roam almost wild on the ranges.

They usually ride a *Quarter Horse**, which is famous for its great speed.
- In Argentina, cowboys are called **gauchos**, and they ride Criollo horses.

In Mexico they are called **vaqueros**, and they ride mustangs.
- Australian **stockmen** usually ride Walers, which are strong horses originally bred by the early settlers.

Ranching terms

Here are some of the most common ranching terms.
- A **remuda** is a term used in the states of the western U.S.A. for a herd of *broken** horses which are used for working on a ranch.

- A **cutting horse** is a type of pony which has been trained to **cut out**, or separate, animals from a herd of cattle.
- A **lariat** is a type of *lasso** which is used by riders and cowboys to capture horses, steers (bullocks), cows or other animals.

Ranching clothes

Stetson

Bandanna

Gloves

Chaps

Boots

*Breaking, 62; Heavy horses, 32; Lasso, 120; Quarter Horse, 30; Steam engine, 113

For a link to a website where you can visit an online museum and explore the life of a cowboy, go to **www.usborne-quicklinks.com**

Work in breweries

Some heavy breeds are still used to pull heavy vehicles because of their great strength. They are known as **draft horses**.
• Breeds such as the *Clydesdale**, *Suffolk Punch**, and *Percheron** are used by some brewers to pull carts with barrels of beer for deliveries in towns and cities. The horses are trained to work on busy roads.

Pulling a brewery cart

Police work

In many large cities, such as London, Tokyo and New York, police forces use horses to patrol the streets and control crowds.

These highly trained and disciplined horses give their police riders a good view over cars and the heads of people and can move quickly in any direction. This is vital for controlling crowds.
• Mounted police forces, such as the **Royal Canadian Mounted Police**, known as **Mounties**, founded in 1873, work in both town and country. They carry out traffic duties and patrol the streets to keep an eye on things.

Canadian Mountie

• In Jordan, the mounted **Desert Police**, which uses both horses and camels, are based in remote areas which are difficult to reach by car.

Members of the Kentucky Horse Park Mounted Police

Military horses

Horses played a vital part in armies until the early 20th century. The speed and mobility they provided changed the history of the world. Horses were used both as *cavalry** mounts and to pull chariots carrying armed soldiers. In Europe, in the Middle Ages, they went into battle dressed in armor plating. Horses were used later to pull guns.

Egyptian pharaoh Tutankhamun in his chariot

Ceremonial horses

Although in battle, horses have now been replaced by armed vehicles such as tanks and armored cars, they are still used in armies for ceremonial purposes.
• The Household Cavalry Regiment is one of the few mounted regiments remaining in the British Army. It provides the sovereign's escort on state occasions, such as the Opening of Parliament. The regiment consists of squadrons of the Life Guards, with scarlet

Household Cavalry drum horse

uniforms and white plumes, and Blues and Royals, with blue uniforms and red plumes.
• In Nigeria, the local rulers are attended by warriors on horseback at traditional ceremonies. Special escorts and horses dressed in elaborate clothes ride beside the royal party.

A royal escort in Nigeria

*Cavalry, 7; Clydesdale, 32; Percheron, 32; Suffolk Punch, 32

Drag hunting

Drag hunting is a sport which involves following an artificial scent, rather than live quarry such as foxes, across open countryside. A man on foot drags a sack containing the scent. He is followed about 45 minutes later by the hunt members on horseback with the hounds.

Drag hunt members

The sport of drag hunting goes back more than 300 years. But most drag hunts today are no more than 50 years old. The following officers are appointed.

• The **master** or **joint masters** act as leader or leaders of the drag hunt.

Hounds

Foxhounds are mainly used for drag hunting, as they are good at following the scent. They are usually white with black and tan markings on the head and body. They should all have a similar build so that they run at the same pace.

Turnout

The appearance of the rider and horse is called the **turnout**. The rules of dress for drag hunters are similar

to those in fox hunting. Hunters and horses should be neat and clean and look nice.

• A **hunting cap**, or a jockey skull cap with black velvet cover, is usually worn.

• A wide range of **coats**, **jodhpurs** and **boots** are acceptable, including a black or dark blue coat with **white stock** (hunting tie). Also worn is a tweed coat, collar and tie,

• The **huntsman** is the chief assistant to the master. He manages the hounds in the hunting field. He must spend a lot of time with them and get to know them.

• The **field master** looks after the field. He or she must be able to exert authority, be a bold horseman and know the country well.

• The **whipper-in** helps the huntsman control the hounds. There is usually more than one whipper-in.

• The **line men** prepare the **line of scent**. They need to be on good terms with the farmers whose land the hunt crosses, and to know what will make a good route.

• The **hunt secretary** does much routine work. He or she organizes meetings, and acts as a liaison between the hunt and the farmers and landowners.

The drag

The **drag** is the scent that is laid. The best one for foxhounds is made of soiled litter from a tame fox's kennel, or a sack smelling of the same. Aniseed is also often used.

The drag must be strong enough for the hounds to follow it. The scent is renewed at intervals on the drag to ensure this.

buff breeches with brown or black boots, or jodhpurs with brown jodhpur boots.

• A warm pair of **gloves**, usually string, is essential.

• A **hunting whip** with a thong and lash should be carried. This can be used when the hounds pass close to the horse's heels, and also when opening and shutting gates.

Some hunting terms

All on means that every hound in the pack is present.

Babbler is a hound which speaks but is not on the line (following the scent).

Blind means the hedges are in leaf and ditches ill-defined.

Cap is the fee paid to the hunt by strangers given permission to hunt for a day.

Carrying the scent is when a hound actually smells the line when the pack is running.

Cast is when the huntsman directs the hounds to search out the line.

Couple means two hounds. A pack is counted in couples.

Covert is any wood, but not a very large one.

Draw is the area chosen for a day's hunting.

Field is the horses and riders that follow the hounds.

Foil is when sheep or other animals cross the line, so covering the scent.

Full cry is when most of the hounds are onto the scent and speaking (making a noise).

Heads up describes the hounds when they are not searching for the scent.

Line is the trail of scent which the hounds follow.

MFH Master of Foxhounds.

Music is the cry of hounds when hunting.

Speak (not bark) is the word used to describe the noise a hound makes.

"**Ware wire/hol/oss**" means beware of a wire, hole or horse.

Transportation

Before the days of trains, cars, lorries and buses, all land transportation depended on the horse - for carrying passengers on horseback, or pulling carriages with goods and people. People in ancient times built roads with good surfaces, so that wheeled carts and carriages pulled by horses could move quickly and comfortably.

Guard

Early road travel

The first proper system of roads was built in **Persia** in the 6th century BC, to link towns throughout the Persian empire. The main part of this network was called the Royal Road. It covered 2,500 km (1,550 miles). Official messengers ran along it on foot, at an average speed of 35km/h (22mph).

• About 2,000 years ago, the **Romans** built over 80,500 km (50,000 miles) of roads all over Europe and the Middle East. They were built so that the Romans could move troops and officials quickly and easily to all parts of their vast empire.

• The Romans built **roadside inns** which were used to supply fresh horses to the travelers using the roads. Large stones were also placed at regular intervals along the roads which were used by the riders as mounting blocks.

• Early wheeled carriages used in Roman times were simple covered carts. But after the Roman Empire broke up, the condition of the roads became very bad. It was more comfortable to travel on horseback.

A litter carried between horses

• Sometimes rich women traveled in carriages without wheels called **litters**. They were carried between two horses or donkeys.

Postal services

• **Mail coaches** were first used in 1784 in Britain to replace the mail service carried by riders on horseback.

The first mail coach ran from Bath to London, a journey of about 161 km (100 miles), which was covered in 15 hours.

Passengers were carried. A guard, employed by the Post Office, was responsible for timekeeping and for the safety of the mail. He sat at the back next to the mail box, armed with pistols.

• The **Pony Express** was established in the U.S.A. in 1860, as a fast mail service from St. Joseph, Missouri to San Francisco. But the service lasted only 18 months, and was replaced by the stagecoach service.

• 500 horses were used, with 190 staging posts, each about 19 km (12 miles) apart.

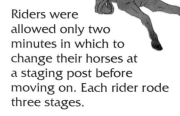

Riders were allowed only two minutes in which to change their horses at a staging post before moving on. Each rider rode three stages.

For a link to a website where you can find out more about the Pony Express and see a map of the route across the U.S.A., go to **www.usborne-quicklinks.com**

Passenger services

Stagecoach

Stagecoaches were public passenger-carrying vehicles. They were like mail coaches, but they carried more passengers - 12 on top and four inside. They were so punctual that people could set their watches by them.

In order to attract business, stagecoaches were brightly painted on their sides with the names of the **stages**, or places, they visited.

Highwaymen

As well as bad roads, travelers also faced attack by robbers on horseback, known as **highwaymen**, who hid beside the roads. Some highwaymen attacked in groups.

Town travel

Until the 19th century, transportation in European cities was chaotic. Most people went places on foot. Rich people traveled on horseback or were carried in litters.

• The first real public transportation in cities was introduced in Paris in 1823. It used **omnibuses**, which were large carriages pulled by teams of horses. They could hold many more passengers than the earlier stagecoaches.

An omnibus full of passengers

• The first public **horse-drawn tramway** was introduced in New York in 1832. The **tramcar** was a bus pulled along rails by horses. It gave a much smoother ride than the omnibuses.

The tramcar looked like a large stagecoach. It had three compartments with seats for 30 inside. 30 more could sit on the roof.

Tramcar

Horses for industry

• The first **tramways** were built to carry stone, coal and iron ore out of quarries and mines. Horses were used to pull loaded carts along iron rails to canals or seaports.

• Until the early 19th century, when railways began to be used, raw materials such as coal, grain and cotton were pulled by **barge horses** in boats called **barges**. The horses were led along towpaths beside waterways called **canals**. A draft horse pulling a barge could move weights of up to 30 tonnes (29 tons).

Barge horse

Horses in history

Horses have played a vital part in the histories of many countries. Once horses were domesticated, people were able to travel much greater distances than before. So conquering armies and their supplies could be transported across continents much more quickly.

Peoples and horses

The Battle of Kadesh, 1286BC

Egyptians and Hittites

The **Egyptians** first used horse-drawn chariots when they were introduced in about 1850BC. One of the greatest chariot battles in history took place in 1286BC at Kadesh (in northern Syria), when the **Hittites** of present-day Turkey defeated the Egyptians under Ramses II.

Scythians

From about 700BC, nomadic people called the **Scythians** spread out from central Asia to eastern Europe. They were highly skilled horsemen and also metalsmiths. They made beautiful gold jewelry decorated with horses.

Gold Scythian comb depicting warriors and horses

Thracians

The heart of the **Thracian** Empire (c.6000-650BC) was present-day Bulgaria. Gold and silver dishes and jewelry, decorated with horses and other animals, have been found in tombs. This indicates that the Thracians were great warrior horsemen.

Parthians

Parthia was a country in Iran in the 2nd century BC. Parthian horsemen developed a battle tactic in which they retreated and then shot their arrows backward at the enemy. A remark said in parting is now known as a **Parthian shot**.

Silver-gilt Persian dish showing a lion hunt

Greeks

Xenophon (c.430-354BC) was a Greek cavalry officer and historian. He wrote the first books on horsemanship, called *Hippike*. Much of the information he recorded is still useful today.

Roman chariot racing

Chariot racing was the most popular spectator sport in ancient Rome. Races were held at a racecourse called the *Circus Maximus*, holding 250,000 spectators. 24 races might take place in one day.

Circus Maximus in Rome

Chinese

For many centuries the Chinese armies consisted of foot soldiers, with only a few horse-drawn chariots.

Chinese flying horse

But later, horses from Ferghana near Samarkand were imported into China. By the 7th century AD, huge **stud farms** were breeding horses.

For a link to a website where you can play an online matching game and then find out more about famous horse legends, go to **www.usborne-quicklinks.com**

Queen Boudicca

Famous horses

- **Bucephalus** was the horse of **Alexander the Great**. He carried his master through his Asian campaigns. He died in India in 326BC and was buried on the banks of the River Jhelum.
- **Babieca** was a white horse belonging to the Spanish mercenary soldier Rodrigo Diaz de Vivar (1040-1099), nicknamed **El Cid** ("the lord") by the Moors of Spain.
- **Roan Barbary** belonged to King **Richard II** of England (1367-1400). The horse is mentioned in Shakespeare's play *Richard II*.
- **Marengo** was ridden by the French Emperor **Napoleon** during his Italian and Austrian campaigns. He was with his master when the French were defeated at Waterloo in 1815.
- **Copenhagen** was the horse ridden by the British commander the **Duke of Wellington** at the Battle of Waterloo.

Boudicca

Boudicca (died AD62) was the Queen of the Iceni in England. She is thought to have been the first English queen to have kept a racing stud. She also bred horses for export to Rome. In AD61 she rebelled against the Romans. But she was defeated and killed herself.

Mongols

The **Mongols** were nomads from the region now called Mongolia. They were skilled horsemen who, in the 13th century, conquered one of the largest empires in history.

Mongol horsemen riding into battle

Arabs

The Prophet **Mohammed** founded a new religion called Islam in Arabia in the 7th century AD. His followers rode horses and camels when they conquered their huge empire.

The Great Horse

The **Great Horse** was a powerful horse used by knights in Europe in the Middle Ages. Knights in armor could weigh as much as 30 stone (420lb, 190.5kg).

Native Americans

The **Native Americans** only had horses when they were introduced by Europeans in the 16th century. They became great riders and their warriors rode bareback.

107

Religion and mythology

People in ancient times often valued horses above all other animals. They were seen as symbols of nobility, or were adopted as part of a religious cult. There are many legends which tell of horses and horse-like spirits with supernatural powers, that could fly or change into amazing shapes.

Gods and goddesses

• **Poseidon** was the Greek god of the sea and controlled storms and sea monsters. He was also worshiped as god of earthquakes and creator of horses.

Poseidon

Poseidon rode a chariot through the sea, pulled by *hippocampi*. These creatures had the heads and forelegs of horses, but the tails of fish.

• **Epona** was the Celtic horse goddess and patroness of horse breeders. She was first worshiped in Gaul (France) during the Iron Age. Her cult spread to Spain, Germany, the Danube and Scotland, and then to Italy, where she was adopted as a goddess by the Romans.
• The Greeks believed that the Sun and the Moon were drawn across the sky in chariots every day and night. **Helios** drove the Sun chariot, which was pulled by the golden horses of **Apollo**, the god of the Sun.

Apollo in his chariot

Mythical horses

• According to Greek mythology, the winged horse **Pegasus** was the first horse in the world. He was the son of Poseidon and the monster Gorgon called Medusa. He helped the hero Bellerophon to kill a fire-breathing monster called the Chimaera.

Greek vase depicting Pegasus

• **Sleipnir** was a white, eight-legged horse. He was given as a peace offering to the god Odin, father of all the Norse gods. Sleipnir could gallop across land, sea or air, and he and his master had many adventures together.

Odin on Sleipnir

For a link to a website where you can read a story involving Pegasus, the famous winged horse, go to **www.usborne-quicklinks.com**

Rustam on Ruksh

• **Ruksh** was the brave mount of the Persian hero Rustam, who is known as the "Lion of Persia". He helped his master in many adventures, and they died together at the hands of Rustam's treacherous half-brother Shaghad.

• **Kanthaka** was the favorite horse of the religious leader Prince Gautama Siddhartha (c.563-483BC), founder of Buddhism. It was on this horse that the Prince left his palace and began his travels around northern India, preaching his new religion.

• **Al Borak** was the winged horse of the Prophet Mohammed (c.570-632), the founder of Islam. Dazzling white and with a man's head, Al Borak was very splendid and incredibly fast. He carried the Prophet from earth to the seventh heaven, "the state of eternal happiness".

Fabulous creatures

• In Scottish folklore, the **kelpie** was a water spirit in the form of a horse. It lured humans onto its back and then rode out to sea where it drowned them.

• The **unicorn** was a mythical, horse-like creature with a single, long horn twisting from the middle of its forehead. The story of the unicorn is believed to have originated in India. In Europe, the unicorn became very important in Christian symbolism, where it came to represent honesty, goodness and purity.

• The **centaurs** were demi-gods from Greek mythology. Their lower bodies and legs were those of a horse, while their heads and top halves were those of a man. The most famous centaur was called Chiron. He taught the Greek hero Achilles and was also tutor to Jason, the hero of the Argonauts.

Bronze figure of a centaur

Superstitions

• **Horse brasses** are brass ornaments used to decorate horse harnesses. Originally they were used as lucky charms and were thought to ward off "the evil eye". Each brass had a different meaning. For example, a brass of the Sun was believed to bring good luck. They are still sometimes worn on heavy horses. They are often collected to decorate the inside of houses.

• In many parts of the world, the **horseshoe** is a symbol of good luck. It is usually shown with the open part at the top, so that the luck will not run out. The horseshoe's magical powers are also related to its being made of iron, a powerful metal believed to repel evil spirits.

Horseshoes are found on the doors of houses to bring luck.

• A **horse whisperer** is someone who uses a form of body language to communicate with horses and win their trust and confidence.

109

Horses in literature

People's love of horses is shown in the stories that have been written about them. For thousands of years, horses have been portrayed in literature as brave, noble creatures and loyal friends to humans. Sometimes horses have been portrayed as being even better than their owners.

A modern reproduction of the Trojan Horse in Truva, Turkey

Some literary horses

• During the Trojan Wars of about 1185BC, the Greeks built a huge wooden horse, now called the **Trojan Horse**, which they left outside the walls of Troy. The Trojans pulled it inside their city. When night fell, Greek soldiers hidden inside the horse climbed out and opened the city gates to their army. This story was told by a poet called **Homer**, who lived in about 800BC.

Black Beauty

• **Black Beauty** is the horse featured in a famous book of that name written by an English novelist called **Anna Sewell** (1820-1875). It is one of the most popular and famous stories of the life of a horse.

• In 1925, a Swiss writer called **A.F. Tschiffely** (1895-1954) set out on a journey of 16,000 km (10,000 miles) from Buenos Aires in Argentina to Washington D.C., U.S.A. He used two Criollo horses called **Mancha** and **Gato**. The journey took two and a half years. He later wrote about the journey in his book *Tschiffely's Ride*.

Mancha and Gato

• The **Houyhnhnms** were a race of creatures who looked like horses but who could talk like humans. They were very intelligent, pure and good, and they represent ideal human beings. They feature in a book called *Gulliver's Travels*, written in 1726 by **Jonathan Swift** (1667-1745).

For a link to a website where you can write a story about horses online and share it with other readers, go to
www.usborne-quicklinks.com

• **Black Bess** was the beautiful mare that was supposed to have belonged to the famous *highwayman** Dick Turpin (1706-1739). The horse features in a novel of 1834, called *Rookwood*, written by an English author called **Harrison Ainsworth**. In this, Turpin and Black Bess ride from London to York.

• **Rosinante** is the horse belonging to Don Quixote, a character created by a Spanish poet called **Miguel Cervantes** (1547-1616). Together, horse and master had many adventures. One of the most famous was when Don Quixote and his companion Sancho Panza started to attack what they thought were giants standing and waving their arms. But the giants were really windmills.

• The **Maltese Cat** was a poor, flea-bitten little gray horse. But he was very courageous and led his team of Indian polo horses, the Skidars, to victory over their rivals the Archangels. He comes from a short story called *The Maltese Cat* which was written by the English novelist **Rudyard Kipling** (1865 -1936) and was set in India.

• **Ichabod Crane** was a schoolmaster who was driven out of his home town by a headless horseman. **Gunpowder** was the horse he borrowed so that he could get away. They appear in a book called *The Legend of Sleepy Hollow*, by U.S. author **Washington Irving** (1783-1859).

The Maltese Cat leads the Skidars to victory over the Archangels.

• **Bree** and **Hwin** were two Talking Horses from the land of Narnia. They feature in a book written by English author **C.S. Lewis** (1898-1963) called *The Horse and His Boy*. Bree was ridden by the boy Shasta, while Hwin was a beautiful mare ridden by Aravis. Together they escaped from the cruel land of Calormen and went north toward Narnia and freedom.

Don Quixote and Sancho Panza prepare to attack the windmills.

*Highwaymen, 105   111

Horses in art and science

For as long as people have been painting pictures and carving sculptures, the horse has been depicted in their works of art. Many important developments in science, medicine and industry, such as the invention of the engine, have also been made with the help of the horse.

Marble frieze from the Parthenon

Horses in art

• Some of the earliest paintings of horses appear in the **cave paintings** of **Lascaux** in France and **Altamira** in Spain. They were painted by hunting people on the bare stone walls of the caves in about 15,000BC.

Uffington white horse, England

• Celtic culture flourished in Europe from about 500BC until the Roman conquests. The **Celts** worshiped horses as sacred animals. In England, they carved huge **chalk horses** on hillsides.

• The **ancient Greeks** showed horses in their paintings and sculptures almost as often as the human figure. Some of their most famous **horse sculptures** were made for the sides of a temple called the Parthenon in Athens, which was built in the 5th century BC.

• The **Chinese** have often shown horses in their art. During the rule of the dynasty of T'ang emperors of China, who ruled AD 618-907, many beautiful **pottery models** of horses were made, like the one shown here.

• Four **bronze horses** have decorated the front of **St. Mark's Cathedral** in Venice for the past 800 years.

The Horses of St. Mark's

Some people believe that they may have been modeled in the 4th century BC by Lysippus, one of the most famous Greek sculptors.

• The **Bayeux Tapestry** was made soon after the Battle of Hastings in 1066. In this battle, the English King Harold was defeated by the Normans, led by William the Conqueror. The tapestry shows the Norman cavalry fighting the English footsoldiers.

Part of the Bayeux Tapestry

For a link to a website where you can take a virtual tour of the Caves of Lascaux and see cave paintings of horses that are over 15,000 years old, go to **www.usborne-quicklinks.com**

Painters of horses

• **Diego Velasquez** (1599-1660) was a Spanish painter famous for his portraits of the royal family. He was born in Seville, and in 1623 he was appointed court painter to King Philip IV of Spain. He painted a number of magnificent portraits of the king and queen and their children, some showing them on horseback. Many of his paintings are now in the Prado Museum in Madrid.

• **George Stubbs** (1724-1806) was an English artist and one of the most famous painters of horses. He started his career as a portrait painter and medical illustrator. During the 1760s, he spent six years carrying out dissections on horses, and then published a book called *The Anatomy of the Horse*. After this he became very popular as an animal painter.

• **Theodore Géricault** (1791-1824) was a famous French Romantic painter. He was a very ardent horseman and painted many racing scenes and pictures of cavalry. He was killed in a riding accident.

Mounted officer of the Imperial Guard by Géricault

Horses in science

Art and medicine

Leonardo da Vinci (1452-1519) was one of the world's greatest artists. He also dissected the bodies of people and animals, including horses, and made many anatomical drawings. These were much more accurate than anything that had been done before, and helped in the discovery of the construction and function of the bodies of humans and animals.

Horse and rider by da Vinci

The horse as a means of power was replaced by the steam engine.

Horsepower

One of the most important inventions of the Industrial Revolution was the **steam engine**, developed by a Scottish engineer called **James Watt** (1736-1819). He used the term **horsepower** to describe the pulling power of an engine and it is still used. One horsepower is equivalent to 746 watts.

Photography

Eadweard Muybridge (1830-1904) was a British photographer. He made a series of photographs of animal movement. Until then, no one really knew what the sequence of movement of the legs was.

Horse and rider in Muybridge's first attempt to photograph motion

113

Relatives of the horse

All animals that have a single-toed hoof on each leg belong to the horse family known as *Equus*. Asses, donkeys, mules, hinnies and zebras are members of the same family, but are different species. They can interbreed, but the offspring of mixed species are infertile, so they can never produce their own young.

Wild ass

There are three species of wild ass: the African wild ass (*Equus africanus*), which lives in North Africa, the onager (*Equus hemionus*) from the Middle East and northwest India, and the kiang (*Equus kiang*) from the Tibetan plateau, north of the Himalayas. All wild asses look similar, with long, heavy ears, a short mane, no forelock, slender legs and a thin tail.

• The **African wild ass** is grayish in color, with a white belly and dark stripe along its back. It often has horizontal stripes around its legs and a black stripe over its shoulders.

• The **onager** and **kiang** are more red in color and they never have stripes on their legs or across their shoulders.

African wild ass

Onager

Kiang

Donkey

The domesticated ass, or **donkey** (*Equus asinus*), is descended from the African wild ass. It is very strong and can carry heavy loads for long distances with little food and water.

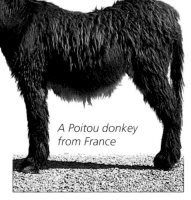

A Poitou donkey from France

The donkey has been used as a pack animal for thousands of years. But today it is also popular as a pet, for riding and for driving, as well as for heavy work.

• Donkey stallions are called **jackasses**, while female donkeys are called **jennies**. They carry their foals for 13 months before they are born. This is two months longer than the horse mare.

For a link to a website where you can find out about Africa's three different kinds of zebras, go to
www.usborne-quicklinks.com

Mule and hinny

Asses and horses can be bred together to produce new animals. The **mule** comes from a donkey stallion and a horse mare. The **hinny** comes from a donkey mare and a horse stallion.

The offspring usually grow up to be very strong and tough. For thousands of years, they have been used as pack animals to carry heavy loads.

A team of mules

Zebra

Today the **zebra** lives only in Africa. Three species survive: the common, mountain, and Grevy's. Each one lives in different surroundings, and has different patterns of stripes on its body.

• The **common** or **plains zebra** (*Equus burchelli*) has the closest *conformation** to the horse. It is the most common of the three species of zebra, and it could once be found throughout eastern and southern Africa. It is completely striped all over its body. Some members have striped, others white legs. Some common zebras have been domesticated.

• **Grevy's zebra** (*Equus grevyi*) is the largest of the three species. It stands about 14 h.h.-15 h.h. (142-152cm). It is the most northern of the species and lives in the open scrub-covered plains of Ethiopia, northern Kenya and Somaliland. It is not closely related to the other two and some people believe that it is closer to the primitive members of the horse family.

Grevy's zebra

• The **mountain zebra** (*Equus zebra*) once ranged from Angola to South Africa, but today it is an endangered species. It is the smallest and wildest of the three species of zebra, and it is very difficult to tame. Its average height is 13 h.h (132cm).

Mountain zebra

Common zebra

Useful addresses

United Kingdom

● British Horse Society
National Equestrian Centre
Stoneleigh Park
Kenilworth
Warwickshire CV8 2LR

● Association of British Riding
Schools
Queens Chambers
38-40 Queen Street
Penzance
Cornwall TR18 4BH

● British Harness Racing Club
Burlington Crescent
Goole
East Yorkshire DN14 5EG

● British Horseball Association
67 Clifford Road
New Barnet
Hertfordshire EN5 5NZ

● UK Polocrosse Association
Ladyfields
Bayton
Nr Kidderminster
Worcestershire DY14 9HT

● Pony Club
British Equestrian Centre
Stoneleigh Park
Kenilworth
Warwickshire CV8 2LR

● Western Horseman's
Society of Great Britain
Llamedos
The Clumps
Ashford
Middlesex TW15 1AT

● International League for
the Protection of Horses
(ILPH)
Anne Colvin House
Snetterton
Norwich
Norfolk NR16 2LR

● Side Saddle Association
Highbury House
19 High Street
Welford
Northampton NN6 6HT

● British Driving Society
27 Dugard Place
Barford
Warwick CV35 8DX

● Irish Long Distance Riding
Association (N Ireland)
188 Ballynahinch Road
Dromore
County Down BT25 1EU

● British Equestrian
Vaulting Ltd.
47 Manderley Close
Eastern Green
Coventry CV5 7NR

● National Pony Society
Willingdon House
102 High Street
Alton
Hampshire GU34 1EN

● Ponies Association (UK)
Chesham House
56 Green End Road
Sawtry
Huntingdon
Cambridgeshire PE17 5UY

● Mounted Games
Association of Great Britain
Ltd
Europa Trading Estate
Parsonage Road
Stratton St Margaret
Swindon
Wiltshire SN3 4RJ

● Riding for the Disabled
Association
Avenue R
National Agricultural Centre
Stoneleigh Park
Kenilworth
Warwickshire CV8 2LY

● British Show Jumping
Association
National Equestrian Centre
Stoneleigh Park
Kenilworth
Warwickshire CV8 2LR

Europe

● Federation Royale Belge des
Sports Equestres
Avenue Hubert des Troopers
156
1020 Bruxelles
Belgium

● Dansk Ride Forbund
Langebjerg 6
2850 Naerum
Denmark

● Fédération Française
d'Equitation
Rue de Tolbiac 25/27
75013 Paris
France

• Deutsche Reiterliche
Vereinigung
Freiher von Langen Strasse13
PO Box 110 265
Warendorf
Germany

• Federazione Italiana Sport
Equestri
Viale Tiziano 74
00196 Rome
Italy

• Federación Hipica Espanola
2, Plaza del Marques de
Salamanca
28006 Madrid
Spain

North America

• United States Pony Clubs
Apt. 110
893 Matlock Street
West Chester PA
19382
USA

• North American Riding for
the Handicapped
Association
P.O. Box 33150
Denver CO
80233
USA

• American Horse Shows
Association
Suite 409
220 East 42nd Street
New York NY
10017
USA

• American Horse Council
Suite 300
1700 K Street, N.W.
Washington DC
20006
USA

• American Horse Protection
Association
Apt. T-100
1000 29th Street, N.W.
Washington DC
20007
USA

• International Side Saddle
Organization
P.O. Box 282
Alton Bay NH
03810
USA

• Canadian Equestrian
Federation
1600 James Maysmith Drive
Gloucester
Ontario K1B 5N4
Canada

New Zealand and Australia

• New Zealand Horse Society
PO Box 1046
Hastings
Hawkes Bay
New Zealand

• Equestrian Federation
Australia Incorporated
77 King William Road
North Adelaide
South Australia 50006
Australia

• Calgary Stampede (Canada)
• Olympia Show Jumping
Championships (UK)
• Horse of the Year Show (UK)
• Royal International Horse
Show (UK)
• Badminton Horse Trials (UK)
• Burghley Horse Trials
(UK)
• Golden Horseshoe Ride
(UK)
• Derby (UK)
• Kentucky Derby (USA)
• Prix de l'Arc de Triomphe
(France)
• Oaks (UK)
• Two Thousand Guineas (UK)
• Pardubice (Czech Republic)
• Grand National (UK)
• Prince Philip Cup (UK)
• Sydney Royal Easter Show
(Australia)
• Royal Dublin Horse Show
(Ireland)
• Royal Show (UK)
• Hickstead British Jumping
Derby (UK)
• Palio (Italy)
• National Carriage Driving
Championships (UK)
• Ponies UK Summer
Championships (UK)
• European Pony
Championships. (Different
countries host the event
each time)
• British Open Polo
Championship (UK)
• British Open Summer
Solstice Ride (UK)
• Cowboy Ski Challenge (USA)
• Qatar International Desert
Marathon (Qatar)

Extra horse terms

Abdomen
The part of the body, in the belly area, that contains the digestive organs.

Above the bit
A term describing a horse which avoids rein contact by pushing his nose forward and carrying his head too high.

Aged
A horse eight years old or more.

Anemia
A deficiency in the number of red blood cells, which may cause a lack of energy.

Bang tail
A tail with the hair squared off close to the dock or solid part of the tail. With heavy horses, "banging-up" the tail refers to tying it up.

Bascule
The curved shape made by a horse's body when in flight over a jump.

Behind the bit
When a horse tries to evade the rein contact by drawing his nose back toward his chest, causing the reins to go slack.

Bone
The diameter of bone and tendons immediately below the knee.

Braids
Lengths of mane or tail hair twisted together. Braiding a mane is done for neatness; to show off the neck and crest; and to train the mane to fall to the side preferred (normally the right, or "off" side). The number of mane braids varies according to the length and shape of the horse's neck. The mane should be braided for hunting, some showing classes, dressage and show jumping. The forelock should be braided and also the tail, unless it has been pulled.

Branding
The method whereby horses (or other animals) are marked with their owner's brand (mark) for purposes of identification.

Breaking out
Starting to sweat again after exercise, having previously cooled off.

Brumby
An Australian wild horse.

Cast (shoe)
When a shoe comes off by accident, rather than being removed deliberately.

Cast (lying down)
A horse lying down and unable to get up. This usually happens when he has rolled over too close to the wall, or has gotten his feet caught beneath a projecting object, such as a manger.

Cat hairs
Long untidy hairs which grow in the coat after clipping.

Change of rein
A change of direction. Also known as **change of hand**.

Circumference
The boundary of an area, especially a circle.

Classical equitation
Equitation is the art of horsemanship. Classical equitation is based on riding skills developed in the 16th and 17th centuries, which are still practiced today.

Cob
A type of horse rather than a breed. A short-legged animal with a maximum height of 15.1 h.h., capable of carrying a substantial weight.

Cold blood
As opposed to *warm blood* or *hot blood* (see below). In some European countries, this term is used to distinguish horses without Thoroughbred or Eastern (purebred) influences. Cold bloods include heavy and draft breeds such as the Shire horse.

Collection
Describes a horse that is being ridden well up on the bit. His neck is raised and his head is on or just in front of the vertical. His steps are short and show great elevation.

Concave
A surface that curves inward.

Convex
A surface that curves or bulges outward.

Cow kick
A forward kick given by the hind legs. It can be very serious to a rider.

Dam
The mother of a foal.

Diagonals
A rider is described as "on

the left diagonal" when his seat returns to the saddle as the horse's left forefoot and right hind foot touch the ground. He is described as "riding on the right diagonal" when his seat returns to the saddle as the right forefoot and left hind foot touch the ground.

Display
When a male horse attracts attention while courting a female.

Docking
Removing the lower part of the tail of harness (driven) horses and some types of riding horses. This used to be common practice, but is now illegal in many countries. It has been illegal in Britain since 1948.

Draft horse
A horse used for drawing (pulling) a vehicle. The term is now usually associated with heavy breeds, such as the Shire, Ardennais and the Irish Draft.

Dumping
Describes when there has been an over-shortening of the wall of the horse's hoof at the toe.

Dutch slip
A simple form of halter used on foals. It is usually made of soft leather or webbing. This provides extra comfort.

Easy keeper
An **easy keeper** is a horse that thrives and stays in good condition.

Extension
The lengthening of a horse's stride and outline.

Feathers
Long hair on the lower limbs, especially at the heels. Most frequently seen in heavy horses.

Flags (red and white)
The flags placed either side of an obstacle on a cross-country or show-jumping course. They indicate the direction of approach to a jump: the red flag is placed on the right side, and the white on the left.

Forage
Bulk feeds for horses or cattle, especially hay, straw and grass.

Forehand
A horse's head, neck, shoulders, withers and forelegs.

Forging
Collision of the toe of a hind shoe with the front shoe when a horse is trotting. This can be recognized by the clicking noise made as one shoe strikes the other. Often noticed in young, unbalanced or tired horses.

Fresh
Describes a horse which has recently given birth. In the U.K. the term is used to describe a horse that is alert and excitable.

Furniture
The metal mountings, such as buckles, found on harness or saddlery.

Gait
The usual gaits of a horse are the walk (a four-beat gait), the trot (two-beat gait), the canter (three-beat gait), and the gallop (four-beat gait). Others include the stepping pace (slow gait), the rack (smooth, fast gait), and a racing pace known a spacing.

Green
Either an inexperienced horse which is broken but not fully trained. Or a trotter or pacer which has not been raced against the clock.

Groom
Someone who is employed to look after horses.

Ground line
The base of a jump used by the horse to judge his take-off point.

Hack
This can be either a riding horse for hire, or a pleasure ride, or a particular type of horse.

Harness
The arrangement of collar and straps worn by driving horses to pull vehicles.

Haw
A third eyelid on a horse's eye, comprising a thin membrane of skin beneath the eyelid that can be drawn across the eye.

Headshy
Describes a horse which abruptly swings his head away from an object or sound, out of fear.

Extra horse terms

Hot blood
A horse of Thoroughbred and Eastern (purebred) stock, such as the Thoroughbred or Arab. Also refers to crosses between these breeds, such as the Anglo-Arab, a cross between a Thoroughbred and Arab.

Hunter
A horse bred and trained to be ridden for hunting.

Impulsion
The energy asked for by the rider and supplied by the horse. Generated by the movement of the horse's hindquarters. Not to be confused with speed.

Iris
The colored, muscular diaphragm in an eye that controls the size of the pupil.

Jar
To cause a harsh vibration.

Jockey
A person engaged to ride a horse in a race. Or a blob of grease or dirt on the saddlery.

Larynx
A hollow, muscular organ forming part of the air passage to the lungs. It forms the "voice box", and helps to prevent food getting into the air passage.

Lasso
A long rope with a noose at one end, used for roping horses and cattle.

Lateral work
Sideways movements of the legs, as well as forward movement, in which the hind feet do not follow in the path of the forefeet. Examples of lateral work include **turn on forehand** and **shoulder in**.

Letting down
Process whereby a fit horse is prepared for a rest at pasture, day and night, for a prolonged period. For example, the "summering" of hunters or "wintering" of polo ponies or competition horses.

Light horse
A term covering riding horses in general.

Livery
The stabling or keeping of horses for money. Or the clothing worn by professional hunt members.

Manure
Horse droppings, usually mixed with bedding.

Mustang
A wild horse of the western parts of the U.S.A. and the plains region of South America.

Muzzle
The part of a horse's head which includes the nostrils, lips, gums and chin. Or a nose covering to prevent a horse tearing blankets, eating bedding or biting.

Outline
The profile of a horse. A correct outline is achieved when he accepts the bit and he is active and balanced.

Overbent
Describes when the nose of the horse comes behind the vertical, usually with an exaggerated longitudinal bend of the neck.

Over-reach
A wound on a horse's heels, caused by the toe of a hind foot striking into them.

Peck
Describes stumbling, when the horse lands after jumping over a fence.

Poultice boot
Used to contain a foot poultice for treating bruises and wounds.

Prophet's thumbprint/mark
A dimple, found on the neck or shoulder. Some people think it is a lucky feature, indicating a good horse.

Pulled mane and tail
A thick mane or tail that has been thinned. It is done to reduce the hairs to the required length, to encourage them to lie flat, and to make them easier to braid.

Quarter marks
Patterns made by brushing against the lie of the coat on the hindquarters. This is done to enhance the appearance. A comb or brush with a stencil may be used.

Racehorse
A horse that has been specially bred for racing. A number of breeds are used, but the most famous is the Thoroughbred.

Rhythm
Regularity and evenness of the hoof beats. The horse must maintain his rhythm at all times.

Ribbon
A silk or cloth ribbon formed into a rose-shaped design. Presented to winning competitors at shows. Also known as rosettes in the U.K.

Roached mane
A mane that has been completely removed by means of clippers. Sometimes done to improve a horse's appearance for competitions.

Saddle rack
The peaked bench on which a saddle is placed for support during cleaning. Or a horse trained for riding.

Schooling
The training and educating of a horse.

School movements
Training exercises during a horse's schooling.

Season
When a mare is ready to mate, she is described as being "in season".

Shed (coat)
To lose the winter or summer coat.

Shying
When a horse swerves away suddenly in fear from an unfamiliar obstacle, sound or smell.

Silage
A crop that is harvested for food while green and kept tender by part fermentation in a silo.

Sire
The father of a foal. (See *dam* above).

Species
The group to which an animal belongs. The horse species is called *Equus caballus.*

Spooky
A term describing something that frightens a horse.

Spore
A kind of cell that can reproduce. Ferns, mosses and molds produce spores.

Standing off (jumping)
When a horse takes off too far away from a jump.

Star gazer
A horse that carries his head unnaturally high.

Tracking up
When a horse's hind feet step into the imprints of his forefeet. He is said to "over track" when the hind feet are placed in front of the prints left by the front feet.

Trailer
A vehicle without an engine used to transport horses by road, and pulled by a towing vehicle. Motorized vehicles are called floats or horsevans. In the U.K. they are known as horseboxes or lorries.

Turned out
A term used to describe when a horse is put out to pasture, not stabled.

Twitch
A loop of cord used to control a horse. It is drawn tight around his upper lip. Twitches should be used as little as possible.

Vices
Unpleasant and sometimes dangerous habits, such as kicking, biting, cribbing. These can be shown by a horse which has been badly handled or kept.

Waist
The waist of a saddle is the narrowest part, immediately behind the head.

Warm blood
In an historic context, warm blood refers to evolutionary theories which suggest that after the last Ice Age, the horse family split into two groups: Northern or "cold-blooded" types (from which heavy breeds developed), and Southern or "warm-blooded" types from which the modern riding horse developed. It also describes a popular type of light sports horse which is a mixture of cold and hot blood breeds.

Whorl
A change in direction of the growth of a horse's coat hair. It forms a circular or irregular pattern, usually found on the head, neck, chest and flanks.

Wrangler
This is a term which is sometimes used in the U.S.A. to describe a cowhand or cowboy.

Index

Index

Index